The Healer and The Healed

The Healer and The Healed

AN EXPLORATION INTO THE ANALYST–ANALYSAND PATTERNING IN DORIS LESSING'SSELF REPRESENTATIONAL NOVELS ANDAUTOBIOGRAPHIES

Sajeesh S

SMART MOVES E 5/11, 2nd Floor, Bitten Market Bhopal, (M.P),India

Contents

Book Title: The Healer and The Healed: An Exploration into the Analyst-Analysand Patterning in Doris Lessing's Self Representational Novels and Autobiographies
Book Author: Sajeesh.S
Published by SMART MOVES
Full postal address: E 5/11, 2nd Floor, Bitten Market, Bhopal, M.P, India
Printed and bound by SMART MOVES
Full postal address: E 5/11, 2nd Floor, Bitten Market, Bhopal, M.P, India
This edition published in: 2018
p-ISBN- 978-81-935930-4-2
Copyright ©2018 By Sajeesh. S

SMART MOVES

India. USA.

ISBN xxx-x-xxxxx-xx-x

Declaration

Certificate

This is to certify that the dissertation titled **The Healer and the Healed: An Exploration into the Analyst-Analysand Patterning in Doris Lessing's Self Representational Novels and Autobiographies** is a record of original Studies and bona fide research carried out by Sri. Sajeesh.S., under my guidance and supervision, and that no part of this thesis has been presented earlier for the award of any degree, diploma, title or recognition.

Dr.G. Koshy
Associate Professor
Dpt. of English
Mar Thoma College,
Tiruvalla, Kerala.

Date:

List of Abbreviations USED

UMS	-	*Under My Skin*
MS	-	*The Memoirs of a Survivor*
The Memoirs	-	*The Memoirs of a Survivor*
GN	-	*The Golden Notebook*
SBD	-	*The Summer Before the Dark*
AE	-	*Alfred and Emily*

Acknowledgements

I thank and praise my almighty God for His abundant grace andmercy thathave sustained me hitherto. I am also indebted to all who have prayed andencouraged me.

I am greatly indebted to my research guide Dr. G. Koshy, Associate Professor, Dept. of English, MarThoma College, Tiruvalla, for his relentless trust in me, and forproviding constant inspiration and guidance, valuable suggestionsand great insights.I thankfully remember his great patience and utmost care while reading and editing the scripts several times, which in fact consumed much of his valuable time. I also remember with great gratitude his wife Dr. Annie Susan Mathew for her valuable suggestions encouragement since the beginning of this research.

I thank the management and staff of Mar Thoma College who offered all facilities to carry out my full-time research studies in the centre. I am grateful to the suggestions and help of Dr. Alex Mathew, the principal. Similarly I am grateful to the timely support and advice from the former principals of Mar Thoma College.

I convey my gratitude to Dr. Elizebeth. J.Thomas, head of the English department, Mar Thoma College, for her timely help. Similarly I am grateful to the teachers in the same department for their helps and encouragement.

I also extend my gratitude to the librarians and staff of the libraries where I found my resources: CIEFLLibrary-Hyderabad British LibraryThiruvanamthapuram, MG University Library Kottayam, Mar Thoma College Library Tiruvalla, UTC LibraryBangalore.

Finally, I am honoured to acknowledge my parents' continuous motivation and prayer that realized a great dream of mine. I owe my deep gratitude to them.

Sajeesh.S

1

Introduction

Psychoanalytic concepts have greatly contributed to the study of literature. The vice versa is also true. For example, psychopathological characters in literature create enormous interest in the study of psychoanalysis. Freud, the father of psychoanalysis, admits that the new method of analyzing the human mind which he has introduced had already been used by poets and philosophers in their works (Simmons 154). He alsostates that literary works, like dreams, express the secret unconscious desires and anxieties of the author; in that way they are manifestations of the author's own neuroses. He relates the creative act of writingto psychoanalytic theory, and thereby probed into the life and works of famous artists. He also enquires whether the writer's neuroses might be linked tohis psychic make-up, as manifested in his work. Freud's brilliant essay onDostoevsky's *Brothers Karamazov* is an early example in this category. Keeping Freud's essay as a model, streams of essays were written by analysts and psychiatrists that mostly focused on individual writers. Among the better-known practitioners were C. G. Jung, Marie Bonaparte, Phyllis Greenacre, Erich Fromm, Henry Rosenzweig, Henry Murray, Selma Freiberg, Ernest Kris, Ernest Jones, and Theodore Reik. Theirwritings contain many remarkable insights into the lives and works of their subjects, and they

6

add substantially to that store of information and perception that lies behind all good critical writing.

To cite a few works as examples for the above category, Ernest Joneswrote an excellent essay on *Hamlet,* which is now regarded as one of the best exercises in psychoanalytic interpretation. In his essay *Hamlet and Oedipus* Jones posits that Hamlet's indecision is rooted in his Oedipal entanglements with his father and mother (the King and the Queen).He ascribes every failure of Hamlet to act to his suppressed feelings of hate and love, and his consequent paralyzing guilt. Similarly, Marie Bonaparte, in her massive study of Allen Poe,*Étude Psychanalytique*, attempts to apply Freud's interpretation of dreams in Poe's stories such as "The Black Cat", "Murders in the Rue Morgue", "The Purloined Letter", "The Gold Bug", "The Tell-Tale Heart", and "The Fall of the House of Usher". Bonaparte indicates the similarity between the structures of these stories to the structure of dreams.Poe's fiction, according to Bonaparte, displays the dream-like mechanisms of displacement, condensation, substitution, splitting of characters, and secondary elaboration. She argues that Poe's stories and poems are filled with infantile attachments, and references to the basic symbolization of father, mother, and "is charged with anxiety, and its power comes from the resulting effects which have re-emerged from deep and hidden sources in the unconscious"(qtd.in Holland 4).

The paramount influence of psychoanalysis on literary studies can be seen with the emergence of psychoanalytic criticism as a separate wing in modern literary criticism. A number of literary critics have experimented with how psychoanalytic concepts could assist the readerin understanding literary works. Prominent among them are I. A. Richards, Kenneth Burke, and Edmund Wilson,whose contributions made many interested in the new approach. The early attempts in psychoanalytic criticism tended to psychoanalyse the individual author. A poem was seen as a fantasy that allowed the author to indulge in repressed wishes, protect themselves from deep-seated anxieties, or both. Marie Bonaparte's study of Edgar Allan Poe is a characteristic example for the above.

After the 1950s, a later generation of psychoanalytic critics shifted their focus of analysis from the author of a work to its characters. They analysed one or more of the characters, and by this, they employed psychoanalytic theories as toolsfor explaining the characters' behaviour and motivations. But not for long, since characters, both evil and good, tended to be seen by these critics as the author's potential selves or projections of various repressed aspects of his or her psyche. For instance, in*APsychoanalytic Study of the Double in Literature*(1970), Robert Rogers begins with the view that human beings are double or multiple in nature. Using this assumption, along with the psychoanalytic concept of"dissociation" (best known by its result, the dual or multiple personality), Rogers concludes that writers reveal instinctual or repressed selves in their books, often without realizing that they have done so (qtd.in Holland 3).

Psychoanalytic concepts were also used to explain the appeal of the work on the minds of the readers and the audience. Thus the literary work has come to be seen as embodyinguniversal human psychological processes and motivations, to which the readers respond more or less unconsciously. For example, René Wellek and Austin Warren included "psychological" criticism as one of the five "extrinsic" approaches to literature in their influential book *Theory of Literature*. "Psychological criticism", they suggest, typically attempts to do at least one of the following: provide a psychological study of an individual writer; explore the nature of the creative process; generalize about "types and laws present within works of literature"; or theorize about the "psychological effects of literature upon its readers" (Wellek81).

Today, we can relate what is in the text, not only withreference to the author's mind or that of his created characters, but also the mind of the reader. This is called Reader Response psychoanalytic criticism. This takes acertain amount of training in most cases, but the critic's job is to help his readers discover how and why they respond in certain ways to the text. He can also help the readers find how their mind filters or distorts what is written so that it fits their own fantasies.

Although Freud is regarded as the father of psychoanalysis, there are a number of other theorists who have contributed greatly to its development. Psychoanalysis, in theory as well as praxis, today does not comprise a homogeneous set of ideas; instead, it includes various perspectives and orientations, which in certain areas pose conflicts.

Disagreements had already begun even at the time of Freud, which further worsened after his death. Freud's favourite disciplesand admirers had disagreements with him on many of his views that actually resulted in the birthof different schools of psychoanalysis later. Carl Jung and Alfred Adler, the 'early revisionists',developed their own perspectives after havingsplitwith Freud in psychoanalysis (Jungian and Adlerian).Both of them felt that Freud had incorrectly connected psychoanalytic concepts with sexuality.They triedto alter many psychoanalytic concepts which were shaped by Freud. For example, Jung redefined psychoanalysis in terms ofhis mythical and spiritual views, while Adler replaced certain Freudian concepts withhis own concepts of the conscious mind, such as motivation and need for achievement as significant elements in psychoanalysis (Stevens 31). Similarly, the Ego psychologists led by Erickson and Hartman rejected Freud's emphasis on*Id* bystressing thesignificanceof*Ego*as the prominent element in deciding a person's personality. Erickson replaced Freud's 'psychosexual' stages of personality with 'psychosocial'ones (Stevens 32).

The object Relations theoriescan also be seen as a reaction against many of the Freudian views. They emphasise that human motivation is directed by the quest for interpersonal relationship, and not by the desire for sensual/sexual pleasure as perthe traditional Freudian view.There are also arguments between the Freudians and Object Relationalistson Freud's view of sexuality as a primary instinct. Similarly, the latter rejected Freud's meta-psychological preferences by calling for attention to the significance of a clinical approach to psychoanalysis.

However, in spite of the conflicting views as seen above, psychoanalysis has developed into an independent discipline which explores the workings of the complex human psyche and analyses mental disorders, suggesting ways of recovery. It would also be wise to see that psychoanalysis of today would have remained impoverished if it had not been enriched with these varied and contrasting perspectives. Of all the disagreements cited above, the strongest is the question whether psychoanalysis is a science or an art. Many theorists have questioned the Freudian concept of psychoanalysis as a science (Green 17). Freud himself preferred to see his brain child purely as a science, which later brought him much blame and severe criticism (Smith 20).

The last fifteen years have witnessed a hermeneutic turn in psychoanalysis. The hermeneutic approach regards psychoanalysis as an art. Moreover, modern hermenueticians see psychoanalysis as an interpretive discipline, which is much akin to literary criticism(Smith 22). Originally, hermeneutics was developed as an independent discipline focussing on Biblical interpretation, and then, interpreting Greek literary works. However, modern hermeneutics has developed as an interdisciplinary approach for interpreting almost all human activities. Modern hermeneutics is interrelated with many other disciplines such as history, culture, linguistics, literature and psychoanalysis. Since the introduction of hermeneutic ideas, psychoanalysis and psychotherapy have come to be seen within the hermeneutic circle as interpretation-making processes, which interconnect an individual with his/her society, culture, language, history, narrative, and self.

The introduction of hermeneutics in psychoanalysis has revived a popular interest in narrative concepts. Lynne Angus comments that, "over the last 10 years, the 'narrative turn' in philosophy, psychology, and social science has had an important impact on the field of psychotherapy" (9). This narrative interest in psychotherapy can be seen in the writings of philosophers such as Paul Ricoeur, Michel Foucault, and Alasdair Macintyre (Angus 9). However, serious attention towards this subject was drawn in the 1990s through the writings of Jerome Bruner, Miller Mair, Donald Polkinghorne and Theodore Sarbin. They have explored the function of various narrative aspects as significant factors in the client-therapist discourse in psychotherapy.

The significant concept in narrative psychology is the individual *self*. Each person owns a unique self; and it is constructed in the form of a story. Since *self* is constructed as a story it can only be conceptualised through the act of narration. A person may hold different versions of his/her *self*. Jerome Bruner says:

> We constantly construct and reconstruct our *selves* to meet the needs of the situations we encounter, and we do so with the guidance of our memories of the past and our hopes and fears of the future. Telling oneself about oneself is like making up a story about who and what we are, what's happened, and why we are doing what we are doing.(12)

Next, the very concept of the *self* is a *text*. As a text provides meaning when it is interpreted, the self also needs to be interpreted. Just like atext that invites different and contrasting interpretations, and thereby differing meanings, so the individual *self* too provides alternative interpretations, and contradictory meanings in varying contexts. For example, in psychotherapy, which is set in the clinical context, a therapist listens to a client's life story while the client is encouraged to narrate his/her life. Here, the client is free to narrate his/her life differently in different contexts in accordance with his/her mood, self-esteem and many other factors that determine the context. Thus, as meaning differs from context to context, each attempts at self-narration creates a re-narrating effect. This possibly creates alterations again, while on many occasions, the therapist and client together participate in the self-story interpretation.

Narrative psychotherapy (treated in detail in the second chapter) emphasises certain narrative strategies in therapy. First of all, it stresses the significance of communication in psychotherapy. For example, psychotherapy consists largely of the analysand's personal narratives. Thus, the therapy relies almost entirely on the communicatory functions of language. In fact, language has much to do with the whole psychotherapeutic processes like resistance, defence, transference and counter transference (Evelyne 56). In therapy, a client narrates his/her *life-story*. Here, *life stories* are seen as linguistic expressions or presentations of the clients' understanding of the meanings of their life events. Thus, the *self-story* or *life-story* should have a definite plot structure, with a beginning, middle and end. A person is considered psychologically healthy as long as he/she can narrate a coherent, complete and meaningful life story. On the other hand, the person is considered psychologically unhealthy if he/she fails to link gaps, to solve inconsistencies, and create meaning in self-narration.

Secondly, narrative psychology emphasizes the dynamics of narration. It sees that the *self* actualises its meaning through the act of narration. In an analytic session the client is left free to narrate his/her *life story*, the way he/she likes. Consequently, in each attempt, the client may create alterations in the story, which may invite different and contrasting interpretations. Here the therapist's role is to act as a co-constructor who helps the client to re-construct his/her life story to one which is more meaningful and more morally superior. Thus, all the narrative aspects like narration, re-narration, telling, and re-telling all play a vital role in therapy.Unlike the conventional concepts of psychoanalysis and psychotherapy, narrative therapy does not stigmatise a person as depressed or anorexic. Perhaps, narrative psychotherapy can be regarded as an offshoot of the 'antipsychiatry movement'. Its view is more humanistic, and it values human beings as individuals, with their own unique selves.

However, the soundness of the self-story can be affected. For instance, the individual's ability to construct a wholeself-story can be interrupted. Sometimes, a person may suffer psychologically as he/she lacks a meaningful self-story. The goal of narrative therapy is to help a person to re-construct his/her self through the act of re-narration. Thus, in narrative psychology,*recovery* means *re-authoring* of the *self*, and many times, recovery takes place through the act of 'self change'(Freeman80-112).

The prime theme of all autobiographical writings is the quest for *selfhood*. Autobiographical writings are both confessional and therapeutic. In narrative psychology, the term *autobiography* has a wide reference. It considers human consciousness as self-reflective, and thus each individual is able to recollect, interpret, restructure and reformulatehis/her life events. Thus, each individual is an autobiographical subject who is able to conceive his/her subjective 'I' experiences creatively.

A person can conceive and narrate his/her experiences and life events only in the form of a story. This story telling is common in all autobiographical narrations. But, all narration ends with the death of the subject, and thus all autobiographies are ended and not completed. An autobiographer cannot depend solely on memory to recollect the past, but he/she has to search the truth of the self in its temporal and moral dimensions. He/she has to validate the meaningfulness and the moral perfection of the self-story, thus, differentiating what is important and what is unimportant. An autobiographer also constructs and reconstructs, interprets and reinterprets his/her life story through the process of 'self-narration'.

The proposed study would inquire into the reciprocal relationship between writing and therapy. On the one hand, the study would throw light on the therapeutic possibilities of self-writing. On the other hand, autobiographical study would become more intelligible while considering autobiographic writing as a therapeutic strategy.

Narrative psychotherapy promotes self-narratives which can either be written or spoken. Two important factors the present study intends to tackle are: the therapeutic purpose behind self-representational writings, and the act of therapeutic 'self narration' contained in them. The present work focuses on the process of self-representational writing, and therefore its attention is on the individual who constructs his/her autobiography. Moreover, this work enquires into the significance of narration in constructing selfhood, an important goal of all self-representational writings. Two important elements discussed in this area are the working of memory and the mixing of fact and fiction. The general term *self representational writings* here refers to pure autobiographies and memoirs and fictional autobiographies.Amore inclusive term *self-representational* is used here to represent all the sub-genres of autobiography. Careful attention has been given to the writings of the autobiographical critics who have attempted to isolate the sub-genres of biography and autobiography.

M.H Abrams considers *autobiography, memoir* and *journal*as the sub-genres of biography:

> *Autobiography* is a biography written by the subject about himself or herself. It is to be distinguished from *memoir*, in which the emphasis is not on the author's developing self but on the people and events that the author has known or witnessed, and also from the private *diary*or *journal* which is a day-to-day record of events in one's life, written for personal use and satisfaction, with little or no thought of publication (emphasis added).(31)

Although Abrams succeeds in separating the memoir and the journal from autobiography by identifying their differences from the latter, it is Philippe Lejeune and Helene Buss who have attempted separating the pure form of autobiography from its fictional variants.Lejeune uses the term "autobiographic pact"for differentiating the pure autobiography from its fictional variants such as the autobiographical novel and the 'fictional autobiography'. By'pact' he meant a contract of identity among the author, the narrator and the protagonist. Lejeune defines autobiography as a "contractual genre", which rests upon the author's guarantee of *identity*: "('identicalness') of the name (author-narrator-protagonist)" (14).He says, "In order for there to be autobiography...the *author*, the *narrator*, and the *protagonist* must be identical" (emphasis added) (14). He continues to say that"the autobiographical pact is the affirmation in the text of this identity, referring back in the final analysis to the *name* of the author on the cover" (emphasis added) (14). The validity of the autobiographical contract, then, isensured by a shared proper name in common to the author, narrator, and protagonist, which can be legally verified. Thus, he defines autobiography as a"retrospective prose narrative written by a real person concerning his own existence, where the focus is his individual life, in particular the story of his personality" (4).On the other hand, Lejeunenotes that "the autobiographic pact" is absentin autobiographical novels. He defines autobiographical novels as"all fictional texts in which the reader has reason to suspect, from theresemblances that he thinks he sees, that there is identity of *author* and*protagonist*"(emphasis added) (13).

Similarly, Helene Buss differentiates pure autobiography from its fictional variants by verifying the 'autobiographic contract' as offered by the author in the title of the text. She says that"autobiography offers a different contract with the reader, a guarantee that the writer is taking the risk of offering a revelation of some part of her/ his own personal life" (6). The 'autobiographical contract', which the writer makes with his/her readers, guarantees that the writer is taking the risk of offering a revelation of her/his own personal life(Buss 6).

On the contrary, she says that instead of the 'autobiographical contract' the writer offers a'fictional contract', which does not offer the guarantee of truth in fictional works, and here the author is under no obligation to reveal the sources of his/her material, and the reader is not licensed to identify fictional characters and events with those from the author's life, however similar they may appear (7). However, she agrees that the 'autobiographical contract as promised in the text does not necessarily restrict the writer from exploring fiction in his/her autobiography (6-7).

Besides 'the autobiographic novel' as defined by Lejuene, Buss identifies two more fictional variants of autobiography, namely 'autobiographical fiction' and 'fictional autobiography' by using the tool of 'autobiographic contract'. 'Autobiographical fiction' is a fictional work that is loosely based on characters or events from an author's life but retains a fictional reading contract i.e. the author denies the reader the guarantee that he/she is "revealing some part of her/his own personal life"(61).On the other hand, 'fictional autobiography' is a fictional work which is written in the form of an autobiography. The narrative may or may not resemble the life story of the author, but once again the fictional contract applies, rather than the autobiographical contract (61).

Along with considering the therapeutic implications in autobiographical writing, this work attempts to formulate the analyst-analysand patterning, first in autobiography, and then in fiction.Thus, adequate attention has been given to exploring this significant relationship and its role in producing the rapeutic result. The second chapter, which discusses the theoretical background of the present study, explores in detail the significance of this therapeutic alliance in psychotherapy, and its application in writing.What causes therapeutic results in psychotherapy still remains a perplexing question among psychotherapists. The majority of the theorists agree that it is the analytical alliance between the client and the therapist which works as the cause behind the therapeutic results.

Many thinkers have studied this miraculous relationship. Of them, the contributions of Sardona Ferenczi remain far superior, especially among his contemporaries. He can be regarded as the pioneer in the area, who later inspired many theorists to research this field. According to him, even the everyday interpersonal relationships could act like therapeutic alliance created between the analyst and the analysand in the clinical atmosphere(Green 9-12). Interpersonal alliance, and the resulting self-healing look similar to the 'individuation process' as discussed by Carl Jung(Storr81). Another significant personality who researched the significance of interpersonal alliance is Harry Stack Sullivan. His investigation, along with the observations of Ferenczi, led to the birth of an integrated and revolutionary approach, which came to be called 'interpersonal psychoanalysis' or 'interpersonal psychotherapy'.

The present work verifies the application of the analyst-analysand patternboth in autobiographical and in fictional writings. First, inquires whether the autobiographical writer can explore his/her writing as an attemptat self-analysis, which is a narrative technique that works in a similar pattern to narrative therapy. In autobiographical writing,the writer can takethe positionsofboth the analyst and the analysand at the same time. A number of narrative theorists have conducted studies in this area. To cite a few names,we have:Joanna Field (*A Life of One's Own*),Margaret Hatcher(*Centering through Writing:Right Brain/Left Brain Techniques Applied to Writing*), Donald Murray(*In Expecting the Unexpected)*,James Moffett (*Writing, Inner Speech, and Meditation*)and James Pennebaker. Among the above studies, the focus will be on the concepts forwarded byJames Pennebaker, whose writing has emphatically statedthe possibility of exploring the analyst-analysand patterning in autobiographical writing.The second question is whethertherapeutic interpersonal relationships canbe traced out in fiction. Almost all self representational writings deal witha common theme, the quest for self and selfhood.A person's development of self depends much on his/her interpersonal relationships. While some of these relationships act as self-constructive and therapeutic, others work asself-dividing and self-destructive. Often interpersonal alliances can form a pattern in a work. The characters' interactions, intimacies and discourses can produce narrative interpretations. Their interpersonal alliances appear similar to the transference relationship(discussed in detail in the second chapter) which is created within the analytical alliancein psychotherapy(Hubert 150).

Doris Lessing was born in 1919 in Persia (now Iran) and grew up and lived in Southern Rhodesia (now Zimbabwe) till 1949, when she came to London. Her father was Alfred Taylor, who worked for the Imperial Bank in Persia. He was a victim of the First World War; and its horror and disillusionment continued in his life till the end. In war, he lost one of his legs, and it was during his stay at Old Royal Free Hospital that he met his future wife Maude McVeagh, a nurse in that hospital. The new family was restlessly on the lookout for a new, independent life, and saw a seemingly golden opportunity presenting itself through the Rhodesian inducement to settlers advertised at the Empire Exhibition in London in 1925.

Lessing, with her younger brother Harry, spent her childhood in an isolated farm of her parents. The family experienced such a hard life that their hopes for better seasons with plenty of cultivation always remained a dream. Lessing and her brother Harry were sent to boarding schools, where Doris dropped her studies due to her eye problems at the age of fourteen. Dropping her studies was dropping her parents' dreams of her. However, thereafter she continued to educate herself by reading. She tried many jobs, first as a telephone operator, then as a typist, and also as a secretary in the Rhodesian parliament.

Her married life was not successful. She talks of this later as, "I do not think marriage is one of my talents. I have been happier unmarried than married" (Newquist 45-60). Her first marriage was with Frank Wisdom, a civil servant, in 1939. Her two children, John and Jean, were born in this marriage. Thereafter she worked in the Rhodesian communist party; and eventually, she got again married to one of her communist colleagues, Gottfried Lessing. This marriage lasted only for four years. Her younger son, Peter was born in 1947 before this marriage ended in divorce in 1949. Thereafter she left Rhodesia to settle down in London with her younger son Peter.

Lessing began her writing career with her publication of *The Grass is Singing* in London, in 1950. Her early reputation as a writer was concerned with her interest in race and colour bar. The outstanding success of *The Grass is Singing* was surprisingly consolidated further by her African short stories, *The Sun between Their Feet* and *This was the Old Chief's Country* (1951) and through documentary writings. Her writing is very prolific and she constantly experiments with different forms and genres. Her writings include poetry, drama, short stories and personal essays. She has written on almost all themes under the sky. Over the course of a distinguished writing career of 50 years, Lessing has led her readers into several very different worlds: colonialist Africa, social breakdown, mental breakdown, and even nuclear disaster. Always deeply political in purpose, she is widely considered as one of the most honest, intelligent and engaging writers of the day. The novelist Margaret Drabble has called her "one of the very few novelists who have refused to believe that the world is too complicated to understand" (Drabble 52). John Leonard, a book critic of *The New York*

Times, described Mrs. Lessing as "one of the half-dozen most interesting minds to have chosen to write fiction in English in this century"(Leonard 34). Critics acclaim her as the most important English woman writer in the present age (Watkins 246).

Lessing has often said that her lack of formal education is an advantage. In an interview in 1964 she claimed that "one of the advantages of not being educated was that I didn't have to write on the second rate and was able to read the classics of European and American literature". She also emphasises that "there are huge gaps in my education, but I'm nonetheless grateful that it went as it did" (Newquist 5). Writing, for Lessing, is a vocation, a compulsion and a matter of temperament. She told Thomas Frick that she became a writer because of frustration, the way she thinks many writers do (158).She admits the same to Ingersoll in 1993: "I have to write. It's a neurosis…I get out of balance…if I don't write" (240). She insists that writing comes from a quest to understand, not an impulse to teach.

Critics attribute three significant influences in Lessing's writings, the first one being communism which lasted from 1944 to 1956.Then she came under the influence of radical psychiatry from the late 1950s till the 1960s, until she turned to Sufism. Lessing's thinking has undergone a continuous evolution which is clearly reflected in her writing. She is never unwilling to repudiate an ideology which she feels not suitable for the present context(Alka104). Ample evidences can be cited to clarify the above statement. It is therefore unwise to pigeonhole her works simply as 'feminist', 'poststructuralist', or postmodernist'. Instead it would be wise to see that all the above ideologies have had their short-lived influence in her writings. For example, her novel *The Golden Notebook* (1962) was proclaimed as a feminist classic in English Literature. However, Lessing expresses her disappointment in being pictured as a feminist and her novel unjustly interpreted as a feminist work. Similarly, her affinity towards communist ideology, as suggested in herearly works, made many of her readersidentify her as a communist. Later, they found themselves beguiled as Lessing disapproved of communism in her later writings. In her essay, "Freedom as Effacement in the Golden Notebook", Tonya Krouse evaluates the possibilities of feminist, poststructuralist, and postmodernist readings on Lessing's *The Golden Notebook*. However,Krouse concludes at the impossibility of making a final reading within the light of a particular theory. Finally, she suggests a collaborative approach which,according to her, would turn more fruitful (56).

Similarly, it would be difficult to tell which writers influenced Doris Lessing. She says in an interview that the classics of European and American literature were her sources of inspiration (Newquist 5). However, critics acknowledge the influence of Idries Shaw, a Sufist thinker on Lessing's writings. Sufism emphasizes the non-rational path towards knowledge. Lessing's unwillingness to be categorized reflects her distrust of academy and her fear that her ideas might not stand up under close scrutiny. She denies being a didactic writer, by stating that her intention is to tell stories, to read them, to create them, that do not operate intellectually, or ideologically, but in a completely different mode (Montremy 196).

Next, most of her writings give an insight into Lessing's interest in radical psychiatry. She came under the influence of R.D Laing, a radical psychologist and a proponent of anti-psychiatry movement. Laing's view of madness is contrary to the traditional view in that he sees schizophrenia as a process of psychic integration and recovery. He also stresses the individual's capacity for self-healing. Lessing's concept of madness stands close to the view of Laing. Also, critics like Marion Vlastos and Roberta Rubenstein see several similarities running between Lessing's *Briefing for a Descent to Hell* and Laing's *The Politics of Experience* (Rubenstein15-38; Vlastos 245-54).

In *Briefing for a Descent to Hell*, the protagonist Charles Watkins is diagnosed as psychotic by expert psychiatrists. Here Lessing suggests how Watkins' experience can become as radical as that of Jessie Watkins, whose psychotic experience is discussed in Laing's *The Politics of Experience*. Similarly, the central theme as projected in her novel *The Golden Notebook* is psychic integration through fragmentation. In this novel, the protagonist Anna Wulf slips to the verge of madness. However, through her schizophrenic experience she makes her way towards psychic integration and self-healing.

Lessing's concepts also appear similar to that of Carl Jung. Her treatment of themes, self-quest and quest for wholeness have close similarity to the concept of 'self individuation 'proposed by Jung. To illustrate, Lessing's*Children of Violence* series takes as its central theme Martha's quest for individuation. Highly autobiographical in its treatment, Lessing pictures her protagonist, Martha, as one who craves for independence and individual freedom. She wants to achieve psychological independence by getting freedom from the clenches of parental protection and the isolated farm life. Martha leaves her parents and the isolated farm to move to the town. There she marries but remains unsatisfied. Then, she becomes an active member in a Marxist group to divorce her husband and marry her colleague. Her mental disturbance makes her analyse her relationships and think how these relationships lead her to psychological bondage. For her, dreams are the keys to open her inner consciousness, which might provide her self-understanding. Like many of her other novels, the quest for self and selfhood is the theme of *The Children of Violence* also.

According to Jung *self* is always in a quest towards 'individuation'. Even psychological disorders can be seen as an attempt of the human self to achieve individuation. This is an experience of wholeness. Human psyche has an ability to heal itself like other parts of the body. Again, critics have studied Lessing's works with reference to the archetypal concepts of Jung. For example, Ruth Whittaker in her work on Lessing tells how Martha's surname 'Quest' connotes the myth of the Holy Grail (36). Lessing tackles the issues of the African natives, particularly, their unconscious fears and racial prejudices. Her spirit of mysticism often intervenes with mythical fibres. Her novel *The Summer Before the Dark* (sic)is interwoven with an episodic mythical dream of the protagonist. The visionary journey of Charles Watkins in *Briefing for a Descent to Hell*is also through a mythical world of oceans and dolphins, islands with ancient flora and fauna, mountain cliffs, archaic and apocalyptic cities, mythical cult cites, dark influences, sinister moonlight, violent acts, personified Greek and Roman gods (Keitel96).

Mental breakdown and recovery are important themes in her writing. Evelyne Keitel in her distinguished work *Reading Psychosis: Readers, Texts and Psychoanalysis*, identifies a new type of genre, 'psychopathography'. By this term she identifies a number of writings, which "communicate a bit beyond the margins of discourse through a literary text". She says that psychopathographies focus on the depiction of psychosis (33). She considers Lessing's two novels, *The Golden Notebook* and *Briefing for a Descent to Hell* as characteristic examples for psychopathographies. Anna Wulf, the protagonist in *The Golden Notebook* suffers from 'writer's block'. She is mentally shattered, and perhaps schizophrenic. The novel discusses how Anna experiences her fear of being fragmented. Her internal fragmentation might be a reflection of her external experience. She has to play different and complicated roles in life such as wife, lover, mother, writer, social activist etc., which make her an introvert. She also encounters self engulfment and lossof identity. Lessing's view of mental breakdown is quite different from the conventional view and very similar to anti-psychiatric concepts. To her, it is an intelligible and potentially healing response to conflicting social demands when the schizoid individual is filled with extreme ontological security for his/her own identity.

In *Briefing for a Descent to Hell* Lessing describes the mental breakdown of Charles Watkins, a Cambridge professor. The novel begins with an unknown psychotic patient admitted in a mental hospital. This man suffers from such disturbing mental turbulence that he loses his identity and coherence of expression. The story ends with Charles regaining his identity. However, Charles' breakdown, although disturbing, is a healing experience. He gets access to a realm unknown, which brings forth a revolutionary change to his identity. Thus it is quite evident that Lessing holds an independent view of madness and self-recovery. This idea is certainly radical; and perhaps, it is close to anti-psychiatric concepts.

Next, Lessing's interest in her characters' dreams is similar to a psychoanalyst's interest in the dreams of the analysand. Like a psychoanalyst, Lessing closely analyses the dreams of her characters. Here the dreams include fantasies too. She is able to locate her characters' inner conflicts by analysing their dreams. Moreover, she highlights the act of dreaming as a process of individuation that leads to an individual towards self recovery and psychological integration. Almost all her protagonists, for example, Martha Quest in *Children of Violence* (series), Anna Wulf in *The Golden Notebook*, Sarah Durham in *Love Again*, Kate Brown in *The Summer Before the Dark*, and Charles Watkins in *Briefing a Descent to Hell* go through the revelatory world of dreams.

Lessing had been called "the archaeologist of human relations" (Howe18). Throughout her writing, she seems to be greatly concerned with interpersonal relationships. Both her fictional and autobiographical works deal much with the self-constructive and self-destructive nature of interpersonal relationships. Supporting this hypothesis, critics claim that the theme of the mother-daughter relationship runs through many of her writings. Many of them conclude that her treatment of the above is her own effort to therapeutically analyse her conflicted relationship with her mother.In addition to that she tackles several other human relationships, which include those between friends, lovers, homosexual partners, etc. She seems to interconnect the theme of interpersonal relationship with another significant theme, the development of individual self, selfhood, and identity. She analyses how interpersonal relationships construct or destruct the self, selfhood, and identity of the individual who joins with another individual in a meaningful relationship. She views these interpersonal alliances as a therapeutic force, which works towards self-healing.

The present study verifies Lessing's purpose in exploring these interpersonal relationships within the light of narrative psychology. The concepts of narrative psychology, particularly the interpersonal alliance between the analyst and the analysand would be useful in exploring the therapeutic interpersonal relationships in Lessing's fictional writings.

Another inference to be verified within the present study is the autobiographical nature of Lessing's fictional writings. A number of critics claim that Lessing's fictional works are autobiographical in essence (Whittaker 35-36).In addition to her two volumes of autobiography, *Under My Skin* and *WalkingUnder the Shade*, she seems to have attempted another cross-genre experiment in *The Memoirs of a Survivor*. Similarly, she has put in many autobiographical elements in her other fictional writings. For example, her parents appear in the form of characters in many of her novels (Lorna 22-23).Next, Martha Quest, the protagonist of *The Children of Violence*, the five-novel series, resembles the author Doris Lessing herself, and Martha's mother may Quest resemblesLessing's mother Emily Maude McVeagh. The predominant theme of this novel series is the mother-daughter conflict, a relationship which Lessing seems to explore through her fictional characters at this stage in her writing.

In the middle phase of her writing career (1970-1980), with *The Memoirs of a Survivor* (1974), Lessing ventures out from the clear-cut distinction between fiction and autobiography and the protection it provides, when she explores her conflicting relationship with her mother in the blended work of fiction and "dream autobiography"(UMS 29). The present study intends to verify Lessing's *The Memoirs of a Survivor* as an act of self-analysis through 'fictionalisis', a term which was coined by DaphnaMarlatt in her work *Self Representation and Fictionalisis*(1990). Marlatt identifies certain autobiographical fictions as their authors' attempts at therapeutic self-analysis. Applying Marlatt's findings to the study of *The Memoirs of a Survivor* would provide more insight and authenticity in verifying the analyst-analysand patterning in the particular work. The important characters of this novel are an unnamed first-person narrator, Emily, perhaps the narrator's younger self, and her unnamed mother. This novel also shadows Lessing's attempt to analyse her early relationship with her mother.

On the other hand, Lessing mixes fact and fiction in her autobiographical writings. There are a number of fictionalised autobiographical accounts in her autobiographical works. Lessing's autobiographical style allows her to fragment events, memories, and sensations. First, she uses many fictional techniques in autobiographical writing. Although her autobiography is narrated mostly in the first person, apparently by following the conventions of the genre, her narrator often shifts grammatical persons, mid-paragraph, from first to third, naming the autobiographical subject "Doris" or "Tiger" or even "the tiny girl", as if she was writing about different characters (UMS 27). In her first volume of autobiography, *Under My Skin*, Lessing's narrative voice alternates between third-and first-person points of view, which create a strange distancing effect in her writings. Moreover, she disrupts the chronological order in writing, by leaping from one past event in her life to a recent experience. For example, in *Under My Skin*, her autobiography till 1949, she writes, "in the year just finished, 1992, I heard of five American biographers writing about me" (UMS14). This disruption of a "retrospective narrative" (Lejune 4) continues throughout this chapter of *Under My Skin*. Along with this, in *Under My Skin*, Lessing concentrates more on other's experience than hers. For example, the initial chapter of this work focuses more on Lessing's mother, Emily Maude McVeagh Tayler, than on Lessing herself. Lessing seems to have such an ambivalent attitude towards the clear cut distinction between the related genres like memoir and autobiography, that she treats her life much in the same manner, both in her memoir and autobiography.

There are many fictionalised accounts of events in her autobiography; and critics have pointed out many fictional elements in it. According to MicheleField "sometimes it's nearly impossible to find a dividing line in Lessing's books between the imaginary and the autobiographical, but *Under My Skin* makes one realize that the autobiographical runs deeper in the fiction than is initially apparent" (47).In the same way, Rose Ellen Cronan also comments that throughout her autobiography she frequently states her fictions are "truer than these 'factual' accounts" (11). Lessing comments of the truthfulness and honesty in her autobiography as:

> The truth …how much of it to tell, how little? …Telling the truth bout yourself is one thing, if you can, but what about the other people? The older I get the more secrets I have, never to be revealed and this, I know is a common condition of people my age.(UMS11)

Another characteristic of Lessing's autobiographical writing is her distrust of memory. She believes memory to be "a careless and lazy organ" (UMS 13). She uses selective memory in the construction of her selfhood. She tells of the fallibility of reconstructing the reality out of memory:

> As you start to write at once the question begins to insist: Why do you remember this and not that? Why do you remember in every detail a whole week, month, more, of a long-ago year, but then complete dark, a blank? How do you know that what you know is more important than what you don't?…You can actually watch your mind doing it, taking a little fragment of fact and then spinning a tale out of it. (UMS 12-13)

Lessing manipulates her memories, sometimes by transforming them into a storied form, which involves a lot of fictionalisation. She says of herself: "I was being a novelist and not a chronicler. But the novel is not the literal truth, then it is true in atmosphere, in feeling more 'true' than this record, which is trying to be factual"(UMS 162). She seems to have created her own versions of the autobiographic truth and the reality. What she remembers of her childhood is different from the descriptions of it by her parents and other adults. She tries to construct her past in accordance with the demands of the present.

Lessing's autobiographical style provides her readers much scope for analysing her writings within the background of narrative psychology, which is evident first in her mixing up of fact and fiction in narrating her personal selfhood. Second, she doubts the validity of memory in autobiographical reconstruction and self-narration. Third, she seems to have analysed herself from various perspectives in her different works. Thus, she uses each of her works as raw material for another, to construct and reconstruct, to interpret and reinterpret herself from her one work to the next. Fourth, the mother-daughter relationship has been an important theme which she explores in most of her self-representational writings; and her writing can be seen as her attempt to analyse her conflicted relationship with her mother. Lessing seems to have analysed this, sometimes through more fictional narratives, which enable her to construct a more healthy and therapeutic version of her relationship with her mother. Finally, in her autobiographical writings Lessing establishes her authority and position as the author, which is a significant requisite in narrative therapy.

Thus, this study verifies Lessing's position as an analyst while she distances her different selves for *self-analysis*, and how the *I* narrator, disguised in the form a character, undergoes analysis. The proposed study consists of six chapters. The first is an introduction to the whole work. The second chapter presents the necessary theoretical basis of the present study. This chapter begins with a brief account of the hermeneutical turn in psychoanalysis and psychotherapy. Furthermore, it scrutinises the theoretical basis of narrative psychology, which includes its major concepts, its contrasts, similarities and connections with other mainstream therapeutic approaches, and its relevance to fictional and autobiographical writing. In addition to this, an attempt has been made to trace the analytic alliance that plays a significant role in psychotherapy, and its possible applications in both autobiographical and fictional writing. The third chapter closely analyses various therapeutic strategies Lessing has applied in her autobiographical writings. Attention has been drawn here to verify Lessing's deliberate act of fictionalization in her autobiographical writings as a therapeutic strategy, where she plays the role of analyst and analysand at the same time. The fourth chapter draws attention to Lessing's so-called 'fictional' writings. It particularly analyses Lessing's act of creating her protagonists, who in turn act as their own healers. Effort has been taken here to see therapeutic/interpersonal relationships created between Lessing's characters. The fifth chapter integrates the findings that are drawn out from the third and fourth chapters: Lessing's act of fictionalizing her autobiography as a therapeutic strategy, and her creation of characters who act as their own self-healers. An attempt has been made here to consider Lessing's *The Memoirs of a Survivor* as a fictional autobiography, by verifying the autobiographical as well as fictional nature of this work. This attempt would further throw light on the therapeutic implications in Lessing's fictional writings.

2

Self-Writing: The Alchemy of Self-Healing

The present work intends to explore how far Lessing has used her writings, particularly her self-representational works, as an aid for self-therapy. This chapter discusses the theoretical framework on which the present study is based, and also analyses autobiography under the light of narrative psychotherapy, a modern school of psychoanalysis, which emphasises the concept of self and narration. This includes a discussion of narrative psychology in brief, such as its origin, important concepts, and meanings of recovery. The thrust will be on examining auto biographical writing within the perspective of narrative psychology.

Hermeneutic approach to Psychoanalysis

Whether Psychoanalysis is purely an art or a science has been an unanswered question for long. Freud, the father of psychoanalysis, preferred to see his brainchild purely as a science. He also believed that the concepts of psychoanalysis could be proved by neuroscientific findings in future (Smith 66-71). The term *hermeneutics*is derived from the Greek word *hermeneuein*, which means 'to make something clear' (Thompson 16). Hermeneutics as a discipline originated in the ancient

Greek world to interpret classical works. Later during the post-Reformation Christian era, it came under theology in the sense of interpreting the Bible. Contemporary conceptions of hermeneutics are predominantly secular, and largely based on the works of Schleiermacher, Dilthy and Heidegger (Sacks E. R 20).

The second part of the twentieth century witnessed a hermeneutic focus on psychoanalysis. According to the hermeneutical view, psychoanalysis is an interpretive discipline, more akin to literary criticism or perhaps historiography than to a natural science, as it owes its allegiance to a set of methodological and evidential norms that are quite distinct from the so-called scientific ones. According to the hermeneutical view psychoanalysis is nothing but a pseudo science. Human subjectivity cannot possibly be captured by the kind of methodological grid employed by physicists and biologists. The argument is that the study of human subjectivity is an interpretive discipline (Smith 65).

The hermeneutic view of psychoanalysis brought about the following changes into focus: First, the hermeneutic view on psychoanalysis rejected the classical view of 'psychoanalytical truth'. According to Freud, psychoanalytic interpretation should tally with the 'real' to be curative (Green 13). Many hermeneutic psychologists take a distance from this approach claiming that it is not matter whether an interpretation is true or false. It only matters whether the patient sees an interpretation curative.

Secondly, it affirmed that psychoanalysis works more on intuition than on empirical findings. For example, the hermeneutic psychologist Donald Spence disclaims the scientific nature of psychoanalysis, as he believes that psychoanalysis has no respect for data, it is notoriously authoritarian, and its theories and hypotheses are tentative (Spence 75).

Third, the hermeneutical view rejects the Freudian view of meta-psychology. Freud divided the mind into conscious, pre-conscious, and unconscious. He also talked about drives such as aggression, sexuality and narcissism. All these terms refer to meta-psychological discourses. A number of hermeneutic thinkers such as Melanie Klein and Roy Schafer called for the expurgation of meta-psychology from psychoanalysis (Green 18).

Narrative psychology

Narrative psychology is a modern school of psychoanalysis that developed during 1960s. Critics have traced the origin of narrative psychology in the works of Alfred Adler (Hester 340). Michael

White and David Epston are regarded as the pioneers of narrative therapy. Later, this form of therapy was propagated by other psychoanalytic thinkers such as Jerome Bruner, Miller Mair, Donald Polkinghorne, Theodore Sarbin, Mark Freeman, Roy Schafer, and John Paul Eakin. Narrative psychology is an interdisciplinary approach to psychoanalysis. It links psychoanalysis to other disciplines such as philosophy, social anthropology, sociology, history, narratology, linguistics,and literary criticism.

Narrative psychology is based on its view of the human self. Generally, the term *self* is a complex concept, with multidimensional meanings. It has social, physical, emotional and spiritual dimensions. However, narrative psychology attributes various meanings to the term *self*. According to it, every human being is endowed with a unique story and an intrinsic urge to narrate it. This story is the story of the *self*. Narrative psychologists see the textual function of the *self* in that as a story demands interpretation, the self-story is to be interpreted as well. To many narrative psychologists, psychoanalytic interpretation is more like the interpretation of a literary work, which is "neither true nor false, although more or less moving and meaningful" (Smith 65). In the analytic background, while listening to the analysand, the analyst keeps open the door for further meaning. Thus the analyst invites the analysand to make narrative revisions that supply more meaning, sometimes contradictory meaning; and therefore,the revised narrative can provide more self-understanding than that initially seems possible. The analysand is left to narrate his life in the way she likes. It does not matter where she places the beginning, the middle or the end. Each narration is similar to each reading of a text that may produce quite different meaning from the earlier. When analysts interpret life stories, they retell the stories which have already been told by their analysands.

Narrative psychologists see human self as a story or narrative, which has a definite plot structure.The narrative construction of the human self is significantly underlined in the theory of narrative psychology. This has been emphasised in the writings of many narrative theorists: Oliver Sacks says that "each of us constructs and lives a 'narrative', and that narrative is us, our identities" (161). People think, dream, communicate, and construct their identities in narrative form. Because of people's tendency to configure their existence in narrative form, the narrative can be considered as the root metaphor for psychology. Human beings think, perceive, imagine, and make moral choices according to narrative structures (Sarbinqtd. in Angus8).

As narration is one of the crucial modes of human conceptualization, the self is also conceptualized through the agency of narration. Karl Simms, in his work on Paul Ricoeur, says that "we understand our own lives –our own selves and our own places in the world – by interpreting our lives as if they were narratives, or, more precisely, through the work of interpreting our lives as we turn them into narratives; and life understood as narrative constitutes self-understanding" (80). In the same way, Anthony PaulKerbyaffirms narrative structures as underlying human experiences (40). He says that our lives are not experienced as random unconnected events, but processed and grasped much the same way as we understand a story (39). He asserts that "life has inherently a narrative structure", and "to understand a life is to trace its development upon a narrative thread, a thread that unites the otherwise disparate or unheeded happenings into the significance of a development, directing to a destiny"(*Narrative and Self*40). In his well- appreciated work *Self as Narrative*, Kim L. Worthington emphasises the nature of human self, which can only be actualized by the act of narration:

> In the process of narration, discrete moments and acts are contextualized: they are enmeshed in a history. Historical narrative contextualization is crucial to human understanding. It is because we can understand or conceptualize the connection and interrelation between remembered, experienced, and anticipated actions and events, and because we can situate them in space and time, that the plethora of stimuli and experiences that constitute our lived world (and ourselves) come to have a meaning.(14)

According to narrative psychology, self has three important dimensions: temporal, moral, and social. Self is a rewritten story, which can be actualized only through narration. An attempt is here made to describe the three dimensions of self, and how the act of narration is significant in its construction of the self.

Kerby in his work, *Narrative and the Self*, discusses in detail the temporal dimension of the human existence. He says that "from birth to death, human existence is eventually measured on the horizon of time" (52). According to him, self is essentially temporal in nature. We introduce ourselves to others through our story. This includes both a brief account of our past and a prospect of our future. Our past is inseparable from our future. For example, who we are in the present are inseparable from who we were in the past. In the same way, we interpret much of the past in accordance with our present. Thus, our self-identity relies much on the retrieval of our past.

Kerby says again that "to narrate the figure of the past is… to attempt a retrieval of ourselves through the plane of self-understanding. It is to create a portrait of ourselves, no matter how badly delineated. Without this recuperative act there would be little or no content to the 'I' that I am for myself" (sic) (53).

With the conceptualization of the self, the temporal nexus not only moves backward into the past as our instinctive response discloses, but it also stretches forward into the future. Kerby remarks, "The present moment rides as if were, on the immediate past and in also caught up in the future project" (19-20). The interaction among the past, present, and future is subtle and intense. Emphasising Kerby'sfindings, a contemporary narrative theorist Roy Schafer talks of the temporal nature of human self, which is enacted in the construction of self-identity:

> Human self works in a temporal circle that we move back from the autobiographical present towards the past to define, redefine, correct and organize a coherent and complete account of our past. In the same way, we move forward from various accounts of our past to constitute our present and sometimes our future. ("Narration in the Psycho-analytic Dialogue"48-49)

Thus, a person's identity is not to be found in her behaviour, but in her capacity to keep a particular narrative going (Giddens 54). The integration of ongoing experience into self-understanding eventually claims the centre of the self-interpreting process, the construction of the self.

However, the temporal and the multiple natures of the self are not in themselves divergent ideas. Narration gives a sense of coherence to the various episodes of the self, and thereby a coherent and unified self can be formed. Things change with the passing of time, but our notion of identity seeks to find some continuity in the change (Kerby 37). Worthington remarks that "in the act of conceptualizing one's selfhood, one writes a narrative of personal continuity through time, despite the radical transformation we might go through in appearance and mentality" (13).

Narration with its innate narrative structure of beginning, middle, and end helps to synthesize the disjoined parts of life into a smooth and interrelated framework. With reference to such a framework, the discrete moments in life can be seen as whole, and therefore provide an individual total meaning. However, without the narrative, the individual would appear to be on the tide of fragmentary moments, disoriented and dissociated. Drawing on Haydon White's arguments, MarkFreeman says that "to live without narrative, it would appear, is to live in an essentially meaningless perpetual present, devoid of form and coherence; it is to experience the world as disconnected and fragmented, as an endless thing that happens" (110).

Similarly, meaning is created only with the presence of a larger frame of reference, and an obvious part-whole relationship. The present action needs a context to attain its significance. Without continuity, reference, and context, the life event may not create any meaning. Kerby asserts that it is the continuity of our life story that constitutes the greater parts of our experienced self identity, and that a breakdown of this sense of identity will occur if the part-whole relation breaks down (45-6).

To illustrate this, brain disorders like amnesia can cause the patientan identity crisis, as the person is not able to relate various events in his/her life, which further creates fragmentation and discontinuity in the life-story which the individual constructs. In brief, the stability and continuity of temporal relations are a prerequisite to achieve self-identity, and narrative affords a structure that provides a sense of continuity through time.

Apart from the temporal dimension,self also moves in a moral one. A person wants to feel worthy and dignified. A moral framework not only defines who a person is, but also helps to define the criterion by which people judge the worth of themselves, both the fullness and emptiness. Charles Taylor says that a moral space is the horizon in which the qualitative discriminations – what is valuable, good, and important and what is not – are maintained. We value our 'selves' in a moral space, which answers what is good and what is bad, what is important and what is unimportant, which is worth doing and which is not (28).

It is the act of self-narration that enables a person to construct a desirable moral self. It enables a person to move from an insufficient knowledge of his/her self towards a more desirable knowledge. Kerby says that thus one can understand one's self and one's world in a way that is arguably or demonstrably preferable to what had existed earlier (171).

Next, besides the temporal and moral dimensions, the self has a social dimension too. The emergence of the self from narration is subtle and complex from the angle of theoretical analysis, but the maintenance of self-identity is concrete and solid in social activities established in interpersonal interactions and engagements. The individual's self identity is accepted and confirmed repeatedly in the daily flux of interpersonal exchanges.

Interpersonal relationships are quite integral to a person's development of his/her self. Certain interpersonal relationships and interactions are self-constructive, as they create a mutually shared reality, through which the individuals bask in the warmth of ontological security. On the other hand, interpersonal interactions need not always be self constructive. For example, the lack of mutuality and egoism disrupt relationships, which may lead towards self-destruction.

Interpersonal relationships have a significant role to play in one's construction of the self-story. The nature of a person's interpersonal relationship would certainly decide the nature of the construction of his/her self-story. For example, a person who fails to maintain meaningful interpersonal relationships also fails to construct a meaningful self-story. The act of self narration is itself an interpersonal activity. For example, in a therapeutic session, it is the interpersonal alliance between the analyst and the analysand that promotes the co-construction of the analysand's self-story. If they fail to create an interpersonal alliance, they would certainly fail in constructing a meaningful self-story.

Narrative psychology is against classical psychoanalytical thought, which stigmatizes a person simply as schizophrenic, paranoiac or depressed. By its better humanistic view, narrative therapy enquires into the meaning and purpose of a person's experience in the context of his/her life. It sees each individual as one who owns a unique story to narrate. This story is the story of a person's self, and everybody has an innate desire to narrate his/her story. A person keeps his/her self or identity by keeping a unique story for himself or herself. People are psychologically healthy as long as they can keep a life story which is coherent and whole. According to Roy Schafer, "those whose self understanding does take a narrative form live a fuller and sounder life" ("Listening in Psychoanalysis").

Owing to various reasons, a person may lose the cohesiveness of his/her life story. For example, traumatic life events may remain as gaps, and thereby the life story may get fragmented. The result will be the lack of self-knowledge and ensuing identity crisis. Secondly, a person's moral sense of his/her *self* may become weak due to the lack of an independent narrative. Thus, he/she may feel worthless and humiliated. It is the goal of narrative therapy to help a person to construct a morally desirable self, replacing the undesirable *self* through the act of self narration.

Cure or recovery is the ultimate goal of any kind of psychotherapy. There are different views on cure in narrative psychology. First, cure refers to the reconstruction and re-authoring of the person's life story. During pre-therapy, the analysand's life-story may remain fragmented, rudimentary, quite unpacked, and wide open to various elaborations and revisions. During narrative therapy the analysand is able to construct an alternative retelling of his/her life story. The result would be the construction of a healthy, coherent and unified *self*. For example, Schafer again says how the narrative therapy provides a new interpretation and a new meaning to the analysand's self: "Insights and interpretation fill in the gaps and alterations in the analysand's life-historical narrative, and that they do so in a way that centres on conflict, defence, compromise, invention and other moves" ("Listening in Psychoanalysis"). Thus, recovery isseen as a result of the re-authoring of one's life-narrative with a logical, complete and coherent plot line.

Along with narrative coherence, recovery is also seen as the result of narrative integration. Many researchers have conceptualized recovery in terms of assimilating problematic experiences into a coherent life-narrative (Freeman53). First, recovery means restoring the narrative integrity of one's life story, which may be interrupted due to traumatic experiences. Second, the term recovery also refers to renewing the self-narrative into a richer and more multidimensional one by introducing a re-narration of one's life story. Third, it refers to reframing the social discourses, or the master narrative that once defined the individual's experience; and by that, the individual attains the power and authority to define oneself with his/her experiences and, "not let others define them" (Adams 17). In this way, recovery is an individual's transformation and the resultant new self which he/she has achieved through the re-narration against the culturally represented good or idealized version of self. For example, Hayden White analyses a woman's recovery process and says how her identity changes from one struggling with anorexia to one with a self-narrative of health and well being (18).

Another view of recovery is based on self-change. This view has been advocated by H.R Markus through his theory of 'possible selves' (954- 58), and Mark Freeman through his theory of the 'rewritten self' (3-15). According to Markus, a person holds various selves known as 'possible selves'. Some of these possible selves are desirable, while others are not. Desirable possible selves can be liberating, since they foster hope for self-change; undesirable possible selves can be conflicting and destructive, because the affective responses and expectations that accompany such selves can act as barriers to positive change. More than that, every human being tries to achieve a 'potential self', which represents the integration of the individual's epistemic and motivational functions (Markus 954- 69). It reveals an individual's awareness of his/her motives and goals, and therefore is interactively connected to one's self-knowledge. Therapy implies enabling a person to achieve his/her potential self. However, a person has to create a self-change in the sense that he/she should narrate the self in the light of the positive self, while discarding the undesirable selves.

According to Freeman, self-change is gained through 'rewriting the self' (3). Freeman's narrative theory of 'rewritten selves' draws on hermeneutic enquiry, where, "one's past and oneself is figured anew through interpretation"(3). His theory explains how an individual can rewrite his/her autobiographical memories, which in turn can help him to construct a new understanding of the self, and resist certain possible selves. It does not matter whether the rewritten version of the past experience is fictitious. The intention is only to restructure the past self in the context of the present interpretation. For example, during therapy, sexually abused people can reinterpret their horrible experiences in a more desirable context (Adams 18).

Next, besides the above perspectives of narrative recovery, narrative therapy also emphasises the working of interpersonal alliance as a crucial element that affects self-recovery. In narrative psychology the term *interpersonal alliance* signifies analytic alliance, i.e. the analyst-analysand relationship in psychotherapy. Any discussion of psychotherapy or psychoanalysis would not be complete unless it considers the overall structure of the therapy. Foremost of all, there is the analyst-analysand relationship. This is a mystic relationship between the healer and the healed, which could be traced back even to primitive society. Anthony Stevens finds a prototype of this mystic relationship in almost all past cultures,and says how a sophisticated form of this relationship is applied in modern psychotherapy:

> The ubiquitous presence of the healer, priest, shaman, guru or witch doctor, and the practices and the rituals of healing are among all the striking cultural universals, and it is from these primordial roots that modern medicine, psychiatry, and psychotherapy

have grown. In that case, the healer should possess authority and charisma, provide personal attention, and possess knowledge and ability to restore a person to health. (5)

The analyst-analysand relationship does not fully contain the implications of a physician visiting an ailing patient. The psychoanalyst does not treat the analysand as a doctor treats someone ill. In the latter case, the person who is ill is asked to observe the doctor's prescriptions scrupulously, submitting to his opinions. In psychoanalysis, this relation as we know is inverted. The analysis lies primarily in the hands of the analysand, who is invited to speak (Green 50). The mutual influence between the analyst and the analysand has been a serious discourse in the history of psychoanalysis. Today, it has been acclaimed by many psychologists that it is the interpersonal relationship that mostly brings out psychoanalytic cure (Green 20).

The analytic alliance in psychotherapy has been variously interpreted. For example, Jung and his analytical school of psychoanalysis tried to see this relationship from a spiritual and mythical perspective (Storr 97). In Jung's view, the personality of the analyst determines the success of the therapy; and thus, training before analysis is an indispensable requirement for becoming an analyst. Anthony Stevens identifies Jung's perspective of the analyst-analysand alliance as a kind of alchemy, where two substances combine, and each is altered (12).

Freud first used the term *transference*, for signifying the working alliance between the analyst and the analysand in psychotherapy. He used this term to denote the patients' inappropriate and unwanted displacement of ideas and memories on to their analysts (Smith 109). By the term *transference* in psychotherapy, he means that the patient transfers his/her early parent-child attachment to his/her analysand. David Livingstone Smith tells about how an analysand projects his/her childhood parental conflicts towards an analyst where"the analyst becomes an emotional substitute for mother or father, and becomes the target of the patient's childhood fantasies, fears, desires, and defences" (110).

Freud emphasises the fact that the phenomenon of *transference* is not only projected towards the analyst, but that also, sometimes, the same form of *transference* can be projected towards the analysand. He called this phenomenon *counter transference*. Freud and his successors believed that interpretation of transference is a significant element in psychotherapy. An analyst should have the proper skill to interpret the patient's *transference*, which would enable the latter to probe into the analysand's past, particularly, his/her relationship with parents, and how the present mental conflict is caused by childhood experience. The patient becomes aware of his/her repressed memories and their effect on his mind. Thus, transference is quite important in therapy.

Therapeutic alliance has become a subject of curious interest among many psychoanalysts and psychoanalytic theorists. Among them, attention needs to be drawn first to Sandor Ferenczi, a Hungarian psychoanalyst and one of the prominent figures in the history of psychoanalysis, who has studied extensively about the therapeutic results of the interpersonal relationship. Primarily, he enquired into the cause and effect of interpersonal relationships in bringing about therapeutic results. He challenged the traditional limits of doctor-patient and analyst-analysand relationships. His determination to understand his personal history and heal himself led him to criticize the fundamental aspects of classical analysis. Ferenczi considers nalysis as a social phenomenon, which requires at least two people. (qtd.in Fortune 243). According to him, "an analyst need not necessarily have superior capabilities; he can be stupider than the analysand and still discover in him things which the latter was blind to" (qtd. in Fortune 244). For him, an analytical alliance can be established in between informal interpersonal relationships also. He says that his "hope goes in the direction that an analytical force can even be possible in between proven friends"(qtd. in Fortune 245). It is Ferenczi who spoke first of the reciprocal nature of analyst-analysand pattern.He says that the analyst-analysand role could be shifted, and both of them can play these roles alternatively.

Ferenczi's research in the working of the interpersonal alliance in therapy was carried on by Harry Stack Sullivan. Based on his work with schizophrenics in the 1920's, Sullivan developed a theory of personality and psychotherapy that emphasized the importance of interpersonal relations. Sullivan's attempt to build a *Two-person theory* or *Field Theory* of psychoanalysis was strongly influenced by Ferenczi.

According to field Theory, in an analytic session the mind of each of the participants is conceived as a field and a set of representations. Their encounter tends to amalgamate the two fields and produce a new, diversified but integrated, field of analysis and transformation. Analytical dialogue and analytical transformation are field events, and they express the confluence, at a representational level, of the respective stories and relational network of the two components of the couple. Speech functions as an operator of the representations, and then mediates the encounter, confrontation, and integration of the mental objects in the analytical field. The spoken words heard and given back to the two individual fields open the way to that confluence, which will lead to the creation of the analytical field. When two persons meet and begin a reciprocal field along with their articulations, representations converge to form a single, diversified and complex territory that tends to become integrated and transformed. The analytical field is thus a terminal event that comprises and amalgamates the individual fields brought together by the change of the two analytical subjects, and by their converging thoughts and effects. The process is similar to that of a large lake formed by the confluence of rivers, each bringing in its tributaries.

The determinant therapeutic factor is provided by the transformation produced in the analytical field.Sullivan emphasised the interpersonal framework which can provide healing in psychotherapy. He tried to see a person's conduct as something that is constructed in the reciprocal give-and-take of interdependent people who are adjusting to one another. He tried to see the analyst-analysand relationship within this interpersonal framework, and it as the most determining factor in treating the patient. Sullivan has also viewed psychopathology in terms of the characteristic patterns of integrating relations with others. For example, he demonstrated that a schizophrenic phenomenon is not a random product of neurological deterioration, but could be understood as a sign of the person's inability to establish healthy interpersonal relationships (*The Interpersonal Theory of Psychiatry*28-32). He argued that the mind occurs in "me-you" patterns, which are obvious in the therapist-patient relationship (32). He tried to see the therapist-patient relationship in terms of "circular causality" which emphasises that human relationships are not simply cause-and-effect, but embedded in a network; the effect influences the cause where the pattern affects the person, who is also affected by the environment (88).

The pioneering works of both Ferenczi and Sullivan have attractedthe wide attention of many psychotherapists to the therapeutic power of interpersonal alliance, and they have explored the possibility of applying it as a strategy in psychotherapy. A group of psychotherapists who apply this strategy in their therapy identify themselves to be *interpersonal psychotherapists* or *relational psychoanalysts*. It is Sullivan who formulated the fundamental concepts of interpersonal psychoanalysis. Later, a few others also have added to Sullivans' concepts. They are DonD. Jackson who founded the 'Mental Research Institute' in Palo Alto, California, and P.Dell and L. Aron(Watzlawick 25).

Interpersonal psychoanalysis does not constitute a unified and integral theory. Rather, it is a conglomerate of different approaches to theory and clinical practice bound together by a shared set of assumptions. True to its integrative nature, the relational psychoanalytic perspective incorporates ideas from the interpersonal school, self-psychology, attachment theory and object relations theory. A relational approach to psychoanalysis can be illustrated by its four underlying concepts: hermeneutics, dialectics, mutuality and intersubjectivity.

Hermeneutics

Interpersonal theory is based on hermeneutic philosophy which sees the analytic couple (patient and analyst) as pattern makers, or, co-constructors of narrative that make human existence intelligible. According to relational theory, which contradicts with the traditional view, the psychoanalytic process is not one of archaeological reconstruction, but rather an active co-construction of a narrative about the patient's life, based both on the patient's contributions, and the analyst's theory and personality (Anderson 315-330).

However, relational theorists object to the term *interpretation* as it is used in the classical sense, in that it implies an active authoritative analyst giving an objective interpretation to a relatively passive and less informed analyst (Aron121). Aron sees the interpretation as a creative expression of the analyst's conception of some aspect of the patient. He refers to relational writers such as K.J Maroda and O. Renik, who prefer the word *intervention* to *interpretation* (88). In line with postmodern philosophies of hermeneutics and contextualism, Aron states that an analyst may interpret with conviction, while eschewing certainty and positive epistemological presuppositions (132).

The relational tradition views interpretation as a bi-personal and reciprocal communication process, a mutual meaning-making process. Interpretation is seen as a complex intersubjective process that develops conjointly between the analyst and the analysand (Aron1331-38). There is thus an emphasis on the mutual generation of data by patient and analyst. Aron's use of the term *interpretation* is extremely broad. From this perspective, all action (verbal and nonverbal, active and passive) communicates meaning, and therefore is interpretative of both the analyst's and patient's subjectivity (140). As mentioned above, this usage moves in the direction of breaking up the distinctions between verbal interpretations, which have been traditionally given higher status, and other verbal and nonverbal interventions that have traditionally been less highly valued. In line with Aron's approach, J.C Muran and J.D Safran prefer the term *meta-communication*, and state that it is important to keep in mind that interpretation in therapy is not one person'ssubjective attempt to make sense of something(70-74).....

Dialectics

This is a process by which opposing elements create, preserve, and negate each other. Each stands in a dynamic, ever-changing relationship to the other. Dialectical movement tends towards integrations that are never achieved. That which is generated dialectically is continuously in motion (Ogden 883-899). Although the relational movement places human relationships rather than biological drives at its theoretical centre, it does not discount the importance of human biology, preferring a *both/and*rather than the*either/or* philosophy regarding human existence. The relational perspective approaches traditionally held distinctions dialectically, attempting to maintain a balance between internal and external relationships, real and imagined relationships, the intra-psychic and interpersonal, the intra-subjective and the inter-subjective, the individual and the social. It fits into the potential space between the Freudian and interpersonal world-views (Aron, 883-99).

Mutuality

The classical view of psychoanalysis depicts analysis optimally operating as a one-way influence, with the analyst influencing and changing the patient, and not vice versa. In contrast to the traditional approaches, the relational approach is distinguished by its epistemology, theory and use of therapeutic methods that recognize and emphasize mutual regulation, influence and generation of data by patient and analyst. The emphasis on mutuality does not mean acceptance of equality. The relational perspective maintains an ethic of asymmetry. In other words, although the influences of both therapist and patient are seen to be mutual, they have separate roles, functions, and responsibilities; and therefore, the data they generate are not equivalent, i.e. their roles are asymmetrical (Ogden 90). Recognition of the differences in power and responsibility of patient and analyst are intrinsic to this approach.

The relational view of technique and clinical intervention is in line with that of Ferenczi who adopted a term suggested by a patient, "the elasticity of technique", in which the analyst, like an elastic band, must yield to the patient's pull, but without ceasing to pull in his own direction (qtd in Aron 140).

Relational analysts therefore tend to advocate a high degree of spontaneity of expression on the part of the analyst. From a relational perspective, analysts cannot self-disclose. No therapeutic interventions can be delivered from a point of view of neutrality. In line with Sullivan, Aron suggests that the analyst is a participant-observer and his/her interventions are reflective of his/her subjectivity (131).

In fact, further along this line, because every intervention is seen as an expression of the analyst's subjectivity, deliberate self-disclosure of counter-transference is often advocated as a clinical technique (138).

Intersubjectivity

Intersubjectivity theory views psychoanalysis as the dialogic attempt of two people together to understand one person's organization of emotional experience by making sense together of their intersubjectively configured experience (Orangeqtd.in Stolerow5). The study of interacting subjectivities, relational configurations, social construction and co-construction, reciprocal and mutual influence, and the interlocking nature of transference and counter-transference have a history of being called by different names. Intersubjectivity theory per se and relational theory are similar, but they are connected to different schools of psychoanalysis, self-psychology and interpersonal psychology (Aron161). The relational approach uses the concept of a relational matrix, the web of relations between self and other, as an overarching framework to include the psychoanalytic concepts from diverse schools, which are in some ways contradictory and incompatible.

The concept of intersubjectivity as applied in relational theory can explain and clarify certain phenomena which were vaguely explained by traditional psychoanalysts. Among them the phenomena of transference, counter-transference and projection are significant in therapy. When explaining the phenomena of transference in therapy, relational theory maintains an intersubjective approach influenced by interpersonal theory and attachment theory(Aron 188). In other words, the patient is seen as bringing to the analytic relationship internalized relational configurations or expectations about patterned relationships between self and other. However, because of the emphasis of relational psychoanalysis on mutuality it is not possible to discuss transference and counter-transference separately. For this reason, the interplay of transference and counter-transference is sometimes referred to as *co-transference* (Orangeqtd. in Stolerow 5-7).

Relational approach sees the patient-analyst relationship as continually being established and re-established through the ongoing mutual influence, in which both the patient and the analyst systematically affect, and are affected by, each other. From this perspective, the patient's thoughts, feelings and communications are not only seen as endogenously determined, autistic creations of the patient, or the result of expectations derived from past interpersonal experiences. Rather, the communications are seen as the patient's efforts to deal with the reality of the therapist. According to this view of the therapeutic relationship, patients always accommodate the interpersonal realities of the analyst and the analytic relationship. For example, "anonymityis never an option for an analyst. You can sit, but never hide behind the couch" (Aron, 97).

Analysis of the analysand's fantasies about the analyst will contribute to a more clear understanding of the patterns, expectations and relationships that patients bring to the analytic relationship, andalsoto an awareness of the emotional conflicts of the analyst, about which the analyst has not always been consciously aware. Obviously, because of the asymmetrical definition of the relationship, the positive result of analysisof the patient's fantasies about the analyst is that the analyst can learn more about his/her own psychology than about that his/her analyst.

From the interpersonal perspective, transference/counter-transference interactions are mutually constructed and are never simply talked about. They are always enacted as they are being discussed. Even when accurately interpreting a transference/counter-transference enactment, the analyst will be participating in or involved in another enactment.

Instead of adhering to the object relations conceptualization of projective identification as referring to the fantasies of ridding the self of unwanted aspects along with the enactment of object relations that accompany these fantasies, the relational approach emphasizes the actual interactions that go on between two people. The relational approach considers the patient's verbal and nonverbal behavior.

Many narrative psychologists are interested in the interpersonal concepts, and they have attempted to integrate these concepts with narrative ideas, to apply them within narrative psychotherapy (Anderson 315-27). In fact, narrative therapists recognize their close affinity to many views that have already been shared by the interpersonal school. Anderson clarifies how the narrative concepts such as the self as a story and psychotherapy as an act of self-storying have also been shared by the interpersonal school (217-220). Along with these similarities, both the schools see therapy as a dialogical act in which varying interpretations are possible. Instead of denying or opposing these similarities, they strive for developing an integrated perspective. For example, when narrative therapists adopted many interpersonal concepts, interpersonal therapists, in turn, practised many narrative concepts. Consequently, therapy is seen as a dialogic attempt of two people together to understand one person's organization of emotional experience by a making together of their subjectivity-configured experiences. Similarly, this integrated perspective emphasises the concept of mutuality and sees psychotherapy as a bi-personal and reciprocal communication process, a mutual meaning making process as stated before.It believes that what is most important in therapy is a new experience rooted in a new interpersonal relationship established between the analyst and the analysand. Old patterns are inevitably repeated, but it is hoped that the patient and analyst together would find ways to move beyond this repetition to free up their relationship and construct new ways of being with each other.This is of critical importance, and it ultimately leads to transformation (healing) in psychotherapy.

Narrative psychology emphasizes the nature of self-narration in autobiography. Thus, autobiographical studiesbecome more meaningful when they are viewed within the light of narrative psychology. Moreover, therapeutic possibilities in autobiographical writing emphasise the latter's possible functionas a therapeutic technique.

Critics see autobiography different from fiction in the sense that the latter is concerned with narration, self expression and representation, whereas the former derives from Biblical hermeneutics, which is concerned with self interpretation (Nalbantian 20). According to Paul Ricoeur, life is no more than biological phenomena, as long as it is not interpreted(11). Life or human experience has what Ricoeur calls "a pre-narrative quality"(11). Thus it is liable to be configured by a narrative. As an interpretive act, autobiography is also a linguistic process. It is through language that we become articulate about ourselves. Mark Freeman identifies the role oflanguage in self narration: "Narrative, in short, appears to arise out of an inherent inclination to narrativize; it is the part and parcel of being in time, and using language to bind experience into a sensible form" (175).

In self-interpretation, we must rely on narrative accounts of our lives and the lives of others. We are not able to interpret the *self* as it is. On the other hand, we are able to interpret the textuality of the *self*. During interpretation, it is the text of the self that is interpreted. Thus, any inquiry into autobiography must take into account somewhere the tension between its historical and literary dimensions.

The process of autobiographical writing is a formation of a new relationship between the past the present. Self-interpretation is a self-rewriting process. In the term *autobiographical recollection,* the suffix 're' refers to the past, and the word collection to "put together in the present" (Freeman180). Moreover, the interpretation of the past should be suitable to the present context. Significantly, there is a moral element involved in one's decision of how to interpret the *self.* An individual must decide what *self* one ought to become. This form of determinism necessarily affects what kind of history to write. Again Freeman says that "a judgment about the meaning of the past … is determined by the constellation of events in question"(*Rewriting of the Self* 19). In autobiography, the narrator interprets one's own life depending on the constraints of the situation. Thus, the meaning in autobiography is more constructed in accordance with the narrative strategies that are explored, and therefore autobiography is not merely a chronicle or confession of one's life history.

Another factor that influences self-interpretation is the nature of memory in autobiographical narration. A veridical account of the past in autobiographical writing is not always possible. In the progression from childhood to adulthood, we undergo developmental changes in the way that we experience and interpret events.

Neuropsychologists also have the same view of memory: "What is remembered is constructed 'on the spot' and is not an exact replica of what happened in the past" (Hester 339). Memory can be transformed by recalling and retelling it in different contexts. Thus, autobiographical narration becomes a fictitious recollection of the past, and autobiographyis that which compiles a sequence of stories that signify what the author believes his/her past to have been. Consequently autobiography gives meaning to the present.

In autobiographical writings, past is based on plausible narration, that is, narratives that are coherent and make sense relative to other narratives, whether factual or hypothetical. The interpretation of one's past is not necessarily based on historical accuracy, but more often on subjective probability, leading to what Freeman and Robinson call "pseudo-development" or "mock development"(53). Thus, the intension of self-interpretation is more therapeutic than confessional. How does a plausible narrative, upon which a rewritten self is based, provide psychological comfort?

Freeman suggests that"only when memories are appropriated into the fabric of the self – which is to say only when one commences to rewrite the self by incorporating one's memories with the context of a plausible narrative order – can they be coincident with a measure of psychic healing" (*Rewriting of the Self* 55).

A new interpretation of the current world and the personal past must be preferable therefore, to an individual former interpretation: "Development must be seen not merely as an addition of the new, but... the suppression and displacement of the old" (Freeman and Robinson 65). Thus, it is through rewriting one' self that an individual experiences the progression from a less desirable to the more desirable self.

Many modern psychologists have conducted studies regarding the therapeutic benefits of autobiographical writing. Of all their studies, the most significant enquiry was whether an autobiographic writer can enact the traditional client-therapist relationship in writing. The most prolific scholar who showed interest in this area was James Pennebaker. He developed many theories that proposed a direct connection between psychological health and autobiographical writing. A psychologist by discipline, Pennebaker's works span three decades and consist of both qualitative and quantitative studies on the above subject. For example, in one of his earliest works he assesses autobiographical writing as an excellent form of therapy (*The Psychology of Physical Symptoms* 70-88). His early works strengthened the foundation of his later theories regarding the direct link between writing and how it enables people to control their physical and mental well-being. Pennebaker also expanded upon his theory regarding the ability of individuals to control life-threatening stresses by means of autobiographical writing. He compared autobiographical writing to conventional psychotherapy, and connected this ability of an individual to one of the goals of psychotherapy, i.e. to facilitate a person's ability to talk about, analyze, and interpret past experiences for the purpose of realigning or reintegrating those experiences with her concept of self. By this time, however, Pennebaker was directly theorizing about how writing can facilitate this process. His Later works further extended his thoughts regarding the therapeutic connections between writing and health, and quite possibly paved the way for additional work by both him and others in the early 1990s, which underscores the value of using autobiographical narrative as a way of overcoming trauma.

Pennebaker's findings could be matched with the views of many narrative theorists of his time and later. Manyof them see self-writing, like psychotherapy, as a dialogical activity, and the human *self* as a dialogic *self* capable of constructing an interaction within itself. The dialogic self can be described as a dynamic (voiced) multiplicity of positions in the landscape of the mind, intertwined as itis with the minds of other people(Hubert147-69). This formulation aims at a far-reaching de-centralization of people that is assumed to consist of a number of relatively autonomous spatial po-sitions, in which it is located with the possibility of moving from one position to another. These movements can lead to dialogic relationships among positions in terms of question and answer or agreement and disagreement. In the above work Hubert suggests that the concept of the dialogical self can further be elaborated by examining its two components, dialogue and self, in somewhat more detail (Hubert169).

Fiction, unlike first person autobiographic writing, provides both the writer and the reader a wide scope of analyzing various patterns of both intrapersonal and interpersonal interactions. Many fictional writers have attempted to analyse the nature of their characters' interactions, and how these interactions are integrated to their quest of selfhood. The theme of self-quest, which is inherent in autobiographical writings,can also be found in fictional writings. For example, Roberta Rubenstein has analyzed how *Doris Lessing* and Virginia Woolf, like many of their contemporaries, incorporate the theme of self-quest in their fictional works (15-38). Rubenstein analyzes how these writers focus on their characters' interactions, which act integrative elements in their quest of the self. What she finds peculiar in these writers' interest in their characters' interaction is their interest in finding how their characters engage in self-revelatory interactions, quite similar to the transfer-ence relationship created in the analytic alliance mode of psychotherapy.

The present study examines Lessing's analysis of interpersonal interactions in relationships, a significant curative aspect that she seems to have explored in her self-representational writings. This narrative strategy reflects its similarity to one of the major psychotherapeutic strategies, i.e. the analyst-analysand alliance in psychotherapy. Thus this study attempts to evaluate the applica-tion of this strategic alliance in Lessing's writings and explains how this leads to therapeutic results.

Critics have agreed that Lessing has created fictional characters that resemble her parents. For example, in *Martha Quest,* she explores her relationship with her own mother by creating fictional characters of herself and her mother (Whittaker 51-55). Moreover, she has formed many fictional characters from her real life while analyzing her own relationship with them. All these relationships have been worked out towards a therapeutic goal.

Lessing worked on interpersonal relationships based on their potential for psychological cure. A reading of her fictional and autobiographical works validates this fact. Many times, Lessing's fictional characters encounter transference in relationships. For example, the central character in *Summer Before the Dark*(sic), Kate Brown, a middle-aged woman, establishes a therapeutic relationship with a young girl, Maureen. This relationship enacts such a form of therapeutic transference that both of these characters project their early relationships with their parents. Thus, the fourth and fifth chapters of this dissertation concentrates on the above aspect. These chapters add more details to her strategy of developing self-narration in her self-representational writings.

┌─────────┐
│ **3** │
└─────────┘

Self-Writing and Self-Healing in Autobiography

This chapter examines how Lessing asserts the therapeutic value of fiction in her first volume of autobiography, *Under My Skin* and *Alfred and Emily*, another autobiographical work published recently. As Lessing therapeutically analyzes her own 'autobiographical self' in her fictional works, she manipulates fiction while narrating her autobiography in the above works. In her recently published *Alfred and Emily*, Lessingsees fiction as a constructive medium to explore the lives of her parents. In the first part of *Alfred and Emily*, she uses imagination and narrates how different and happier their lives would have been. At the same time, in the second part of the book she escapes from the fantasy world,and thereby narrates their factuallives, which is a bitter story. Thus, Lessing's attempt to create alternative versions of her life-story as well as her use of fiction in narrating a morally healthy, more coherent, and meaningful version of it is evident in both *Under My Skin* and *Alfred and Emily*. A reading of the two works would offerLessing's readers a feeling that hersearch forautobiographical truth is beyond the literal, evolving and therapeutic. Similarly, this chapteranalyzes Lessing's ambiguous treatment of memory. She prefers a more clear and healthy account to a dull piece of memory. Lessing's self-narrative style in *Under My Skin* and *Alfred and Emily* seems to be her therapeutic strategy, which is akin to the concepts of narrative psychology. She directs her writing towards self-healing through self-narration. More than that, she acts the role of both the analyst and analysand while drafting and redrafting her self-story from one work to another.

Volume One of My Autobiography, the subtitlethat Lessing gaveto her autobiography, *Under My Skin*, is significant. First, it enables Lessing to have a closer relationship with her readers, which she lacks in her other self-representational writings. This is the very admission of the *autobiographical pact*, which differentiates the genre of autobiography from fiction (Lejeune 61). This pact empowers the reader to identify Lessing as the author, narrator and protagonist of the text. *Under My Skin*also offers the *autobiographic contract*, which is a mandatory qualification of 'pure autobiography' as observed by Helen Buss (12-14).Buss talks of the 'author-reader intimacy',which is promised by the title 'autobiography' (autobiographic contract) of a work:

> What life writing allows that traditional genre expressions guard against, is the empowered reader. By trusting the reader with her life, and admitting that the insights of the text are specific to one person's experience, the autobiographer empowers the reader to make her own meaningful story as she reads, fiction invites me into the life of the text, autobiography invites me to bring the text into my life"(sic).(14)

On the other hand, the author-reader intimacy promised in the text does not impede Lessing from claiming her freedom and authority to construct her life-story therapeutically. By the title 'My Autobiography,' Lessing invests her authority by positioning herself as the author of the text. This enables her to exert power and command over the text, while she allows her own silent past to be re-created. She wants her autobiography to be therapeutic than confessional. For example, readers see how Lessing denies the usual self-revelations that a conventional reader would expect from an autobiography. She says that regarding certain things of her life shehas no intention of telling the truth (UMS 11).She denies her readers the honesty that the readers of conventional autobiography expect from the author. She says, "I am trying to write this book honestly. But were I to write it aged eighty-five, how different would it be?"(UMS17).

Similarly, she conveys her disgust for and uneasiness about the public gaze openly, while letting others construct her biography according to their propensities. A person like Lessing would never be happy while her life is being narrated by others. She says: "I read history with conditional respect… I read some biographies with admiration for people who have chosen to keep their mouths shut" (UMS 11). Furthermore, she clarifies that her intention of writing the autobiography is a safeguard againstanotherperson's attempt to write her biography: "Why an autobiography at all? Self-defence: biographies are being written" (UMS 14). She is also conscious of the possible errors and misrepresentations while publishing articles and interviews (UMS14).

Likewise, she prevents her readers from deducing her life from her autobiographical material in novels and from two short monographs about her parents; rather, she wants to "claim her own life by writing an autobiography" (UMS14). Similarly, she considers that it is now safe to come to the day light instead of partial self revelations that she offered in her semi-autobiographical writings (UMS 11).

Foremost of all, she says that there are aspects of her life she is always trying to understand better (UMS 15). Perhaps, there is no other writer who has manipulated her writing, both fiction and autobiography, for inner-self exploration. She recognizes the complexityof such a self-analysis and therefore she resorts to self-writing as a means to achieve it.

Thus, for Lessing, autobiography is a means forself-analysis, whichis aimedat self-understanding. She emphasises this in *Under My Skin,* by stating her intention for a re-analysis, particularly her relationship with mother (UMS 15). Lessing's autobiographical enquiry, especially her search into her parents' lives, their personalities and her conflicting relationship with them, areagain dealt with in *Under My Skin;*in fact, she does the same in almost all her writings.

Next, just like her autobiographical interest in fictional writings, Lessing reveals her preference to fiction in her autobiography, *Under My Skin.* Lessing's preference to fiction in her autobiography reflects her reception of Sufism. Sufism promotes the non-rational and less-trodden path towards reality. Thus, reality cannot be fully realized through normal modes of perception or expression; instead it can be achieved through more intuitive and less conventional modes.

Lessing oftennarrates her story by choosing discursive methods and provocative structures, which further stimulates her imagination to construct alternative versions of reality at various times. This shows that in writing, Lessing uses fact and fiction as two sides of the same coin. In her autobiography, *Under My Skin*, she breaks the conventional genre distinctions by manipulating various fictional modes.

While analyzing Lessing's use of fiction in her autobiography, it would be essential to understand her conception of truth. In fact, truth is one of the important problems she tackles in *Under My Skin*. In fact, through her autobiography she searches for truth, the truth of her *self*. She states this at the very beginning of her autobiography (UMS 14-15).By truth, perhaps, she means-the truth behind her conflicted relationship with parents, especially, with her mother; her childhood, of which she has quite unclear memories; and then, her two disrupted marriages and her own relationship with her deserted children (UMS 297).

Lessing's search fortruth ultimately reflects her therapeutic intentions. She is definitely curious to find the truth of certain significant but traumaticevents in her life. She sees self-writing as an integrative act ofconducting atherapeutic self-analysis. The art of self-writing enables her to recreate the past events,by experiencingthoseevents once again. She says that she has an innate urge to get back to things that happened in her past, of which her inner psyche is continuously disturbed:

> Dreams have always been my friend, full of information, full of warnings. They insisted in a hundred ways that I was dangerously unhappy about the infants I had left, about my father—but what was new about that?—about my mother, and because I wanted so very much to have time to write, but could not see when that would happen. (UMS 297)

Thus, Lessing searches into her inner divisions, and she resorts toself-narration as an act of self-analysis to relocate the disturbing sub-conscious elements within her. To reach at the truthshe closely analyzes each significant eventclosely. Theseinclude both thosethat happened in her life and also in her parents' lives, which she believes to have influenced much of her and her parents' lives.

That therealization of the truth would be therapeutic is indeed a psychoanalytical concept. In psychotherapy the analyst probes into the disturbing, hidden secrets of the analysand's unconscious mind, and tries to reveal it to the analysand. This is often possible through dream interpretation and analyzing transfererence relationships (Green 120).

While constructing her autobiography, Lessing considers multiple versions of her life events. Among them she chooses which is 'more desirable'. 'The more desirable'here refers to one which is more therapeutic. Choosing the more desirable version enables her to value her *self* as morally superior and meaningful.

A close analysis of Lessing's treatment of 'truth' will also reveal that she does not keep the conventional distinctions between reality and imagination. Often, Lessing's readers feel that she blurs the distinction between the imaginary and the real. For example, Michele Field comments of Lessing's writing that "sometimes it's nearly impossible to find a dividing line in Lessing's books between the imaginary and autobiographical, which runs deeper in the fiction than that is initially apparent" (47).

As for Lessing, creating an imaginary version of a life event meanscreating an alternative perception of reality. She achievespsychological healing while creating imaginary versions of life events, which she considers as probable instead of what really happened. Thus, she often attempts narrating what would have happened, which in turn may fix her as a daydreamer in her autobiographies.

Lessing searches for truth which lies beyond the factual. She says that more truth can be found in her novel, *Martha Quest*, than in her autobiographies, which attempt to be factual:

> In short, when I wrote *Martha Quest* I was being a novelist and not a chronicler. But if the novel is not the literal truth, then it is true in atmosphere, feeling, more 'true' than this record, which is trying to be factual. (UMS 162)

Consider the following exchange between Michele Field and Lessing in an interview given shortly before the release of *Under My Skin*. At the interview, Field remarkedabouther autobiography (he had read an advance copy of *Under My Skin*) that much of her fiction had the ring of real experience, and that *Under My Skin* was more like her other books than most novelists' autobiographies would be. In his review on the interview Field quotes how Lessing responded to his remark: "I think autobiographical novels are truer than autobiography, even if half the novel is untrue…*Martha Quest*…I am too old now to put all that violent emotion in it" (47).

Her semi-autobiographical writings strongly mean that for several decades she hadpreferred not to risk revealing some portion of her personal life. In *Under My Skin* too she exhibits her reservation and inability to reveal the whole truth about her past: "Our old friend, the Truth, is first. The truth…how much of it to tell, how little? It seems it is agreed this is the first problem of the self-chronicler, and obloquy lies in wait either way" (UMS11). She admits her reluctance to reveal certain private truths in her autobiography (UMS 11).

However, the uniqueness of Lessing's writing is that she universalizes her sense of personal truths. Many times by fictionalizing her personal experiences she has given them a universal appeal. One of her stable beliefs is the universality of personal experience. She uses it to justify writing about "petty personal problems" because "nothing is personal in the sense that it is uniquely one's own… growing up is after all only the understanding that one's unique and incredible experience is what everyone shares"(GN 18). However, Lessing does not hold always heradherenceto the universality of personal experience. For example the following statement she made in her book*Prisons We Choose to Live Inside* reveals her emphasis on the individual experience:

> Every thing that ever happened to me has taught me to value the individual, the person who cultivates and preserves her or his own way of thinking, who stands out against group thinking, group pressures.(83)

Thus, even when she emphasizes the nature of her personal experience she is ready to admit that there are peoplewho share experiences and feelings with her.

Another characteristic of Lessing's conception of truth is its distinctive psychological nature. She is intensively curious about the elements affecting and influencing human psyche mind. For example, she is so curious of the traumatic events that disturbed her and her parent's minds; she feels thatthey have had a continuous effect on her and their lives. Writingenables her to come closer to the human psyche, whichshe considers more significant than any other factor. She analyzes her parents' psychological crisis as caused by the two World Wars and their hopeless suffering in the farms, which deeply affected much of her futurethinking. In her writingshe makes deliberate and forceful attempts to enter intothe world of her parents' trauma via her own trauma and vice versa. Thus Lessing's writing reflects her empathetic knowledge of the human psyche.

Lessing's approach to her parents becomes more sympathetic and matured in *Under My Skin*, which enables herto comprehend her own and her parents'minds. Herlater works, particularly *Under My Skin* and *Alfred and Emily*, revealher moresympathetic attitudes towards her parents, which appears quite incontrast toher early antagonistic attitudes towards them, as evident in her early writings.

Lessing believes in narrative truth. She has beenwidely appreciated for her ability as a great storyteller. Perhaps, this has been the general label affixed on her.She has sought and found the immense possibilities of storytelling, thereby realizing the truth. She tells of the immense possibilities of stories and storytelling:

> For thousands upon thousands of years, we–humankind– have told ourselves tales and stories, and these were always analogies and metaphors, parables and allegories; they were elusive and equivocal; they hinted and alluded... (UMS 28)

Convincingly, Lessingprefers to see her life (self) constructed in a storied form. For achievingit she attempt sall narrative possibilities, by exploring means like fantasy, dreams and imagination. Similarly, she holds that these means can be explored for constructing alternativeversions of her life story.Although she is aware of the contradictions these versions create, she makes use of each, which may assist her in her searchfortruth. Thus, sheupholds the narrative view that her *self* is being written, rewritten, constructed and reconstructed through her continuous writing. She is still eager to make omissions, corrections, additions, and alterations. For example, In *Under My Skin* she noticeshowmany of her life events which,onceimplied to besignificant, become less significant and less colourful later:

> When you write about anything–in a novel, an article– you learn a lot you did not know before. I learned a good deal writing this. Again and again I have had to say, 'That was the reason was it? Why didn't I think of that before?'Or even, 'Wait... it wasn't like that'".(13)

By choosing to narrate her 'self' in a literary form, autobiography, she is setting out to construct her life-story as a text, which can be revised later by reading and rereading, interpretingand reinterpreting. She seesthe previous versions as raw material for the subsequent versions. Readers can watchacontinuous progressionin her writing, though she is blamed to have disturbed their vision by repeating events and themes often (Watkins 243). By raising questions and offering answers she is keeping a continuous discourse within the text. Thus, herautobiography offers multiple voices created by the discourse among her multiple selves. Although she entertains the freedom of her multiple selves' voices, she maintains a supreme coherence and a well-unified structure in the text. She achieves this by the mastery ofthe chiefnarrative voice that is omnipresent in the text.

Lessing holds that imagination and truth can go together. Her autobiographical style encourages imagination, which in turn invites alternative narratives. For her, truth exists in fiction as much as it does in autobiography (UMS 28-29). She tries to modify her past, by imposing a pattern on it and there by constructing a more coherent and meaningful story out of it.

Lessing holds the hermeneutic belief that there can be various perspectives on the same event. Thus, she believes in the plurality of truth. This has been ruled as her attachment to the concepts of postmodernism by many critics (Tonya 68). According to Lessing, perception, like taste, is continuously changing. She illustrates this by telling how an agedperson's taste of an omeletteis far different from the taste of it in childhood (UMS21). She writes:

> Telling the truth or not telling it, and how much, is a lesser problem than the one of shifting perspectives, for you see your life differently at different stages, like climbing a mountain while the landscape changes with every turn in the path. Had I written this when I was thirty, it would have been a pretty combative document. In my forties, a wail of despair and guilt: oh my God, how could I have done this or that? Now I look back at that child, that girl, that young woman, with a more and more detached curiosity.(UMS 12)

Thus for Lessing, truth is ever evolving, and therefore, there can be no definite truth. She does not show any unwillingness to repudiate any philosophy or ideology which she thought once valid. Lessing has also been severely criticized for her occasional shifts of views as well as for her denunciation of ideologies which she admired and favoured once.However, it is clear that, she has undergone to a tremendousevolution both in her thinking and in her writing. This strongly reflects in her autobiography. Her act of self-analysis leads her to the act of self-revision. Sheconveys the same to her readers: "I try to see my past selves as someone else might, and then put myself back inside one of them ..." (UMS 12).

More illustrations can be cited forsubstantiatingLessing's willingness to change herperspectives. For example, she alters her assumption of her mother's behaviour:

> I was in nervous fight from her ever since I can remember anything, and from the age of fourteen I set myself obdurately against her in a kind of inner emigration from everything she represented. Girls do have to grow up, but has this battle always been implacable? Now I see her as a tragic figure living out her disappointing years with

courage and with dignity. I saw her then as tragic, certainly, but was not able to be kind.(UMS 15)

An important factor to be considered with Lessing's conception of truth and fiction is her treatment of memory. Her approach to memory and her handling of it in *Under My Skin* would further substantiate her favourtowardsfiction for therapeutic self-narration. Her construction of memory in *Under My Skin* would alsoemphasize her narrative strategy for fashioning her autobiography therapeutically. She projects her deep interest in recreating her past, which is deeply felt by the readers of *Under My Skin*.

Like any autobiographer Lessing uses memory as a significant tool for constructing her past. However, she verifies the possibilities as well as the limitations of her memory for constructing her past. Similarly she is conscious of the dangers she would incur while adhering to her memories. She realizes that there are dissimilar versions of the same event, and strongly reflects the assumption that she herself owns the wisdom and authority to provide an alternative narrative to the one that has her stuck. For example, consider how she coerces her memory in such a wayas to recover the therapeutic truth, that she can get away from others'versions her life events:

> Clearly I had to fight to establish a reality of my own, against an insistence from the adults that I should accept theirs. Pressure had been put on me to admit that what I knew was true was not so. I am deducing this. Why else my preoccupation that went on for years: this is the truth, this is what happened, hold on to it, don't let them talk you out of it. (UMS 13-14)

Shesees the contradictions between herown memories of eventsand what her parents had reported to her. For example, in *Under My Skin*sheanalyzes the two contradictory accounts of her childhood experience, the first she collected from her own memory and the second one created by her mother andreported to her:

> My first memory is before I was two, and it is of an enormous dangerous horse towering up, up, and on it my father still higher, his head and shoulders somewhere in the sky... I am inside the heat of horse, the smell of horse, the smell of my father, all hot pungent smells. When the horse moves it is a jerking jolting motion ... My stomach is

reeling because of the swoop up from the ground now so far below me. Now, that is a real memory, violent, smelly –physical. (UMS18)

Daddy used to put you in front of him on the horse when he rode to the Bank, and Marta waited at the gate to bring you back. You absolutely loved it.(UMS 18)

Lessing examinesthe two contradictory versions (narratives) of the same event as given above, but she does not accept either of them as truth; instead, she develops a third, which is a more agree-ableaccount of the event:

And perhaps I did, perhaps it was only the first ride, which I did not love, that has stayed in my memory. The gate is in a photograph, a graceful arch, and I have added it into the real memory. Of being lifted down into the hands of Marta, whom I disliked, there is nothing in my mind. Those rides had to be in Kermanshah, and I was two and a half when we left. (UMS 18-19)

The third version of the event which Lessing reconstructs here is so reconciliatory that it enables her to move to an emotional compromise with her mother, which is alsoa therapeutic experience. *Under My Skin*, particularly the early part of it, is interspersed with two dissimilar narratives: Lessing's ownrecollection of childhood memories, and her mother's accounts of events.

The past is always an obsessive element to a writer like Lessing, as she forcefully comes back to it again and again. Her act of self-narration continuously evokes in her the past selves, and she engages in an inner dialogue with them. In *Under My Skin* she emphasizes how significant her knowledge of her past is. She knows the constraints of memory; and at the same time, she values narration as a rich sourcefrom which she can recover lost records. Of course, there can be gaps, but she seesthat it is now significant to construct her life story coherent and meaningful. She talks of thisclearly:

It is hard for me to imagine such a darkening of the past. Once even to try would have plunged me into frightful insecurity, as if memory were Self, Identity –and I am sure that isn't so. Now I can imagine myself arriving in some country with the past wiped clean out of my mind: I would do alright. It is after all only what we did when we were born, without memories, or so it seems to the adult: then we have to create our lives, create memory.(UMS 13)

Thus Lessing finds that is essential to construct a coherent, healthy and meaningful life story. She also realizes that the lack of coherence would question her sense of identity. She is emphasizing theconstructive value of fiction when she says that she can fictionally create her memories.

In *Under My Skin*she confesses that there are small remains of the early childhood events in her memory, particularly the events that happened in the "big stone house". However, she is not worried when memories fail; instead she compensates for their limitationsby creatingan alternative one out of imagination. She says how she creates her past by using her "novelist's mind":

> I had been thinking, why had so little remained in me of that big stone house, with its big high stone rooms? I was born there. I learned to walk there. And imagined that I lay in a cot with bars, like a prison cell for size and heard large feet clinging on stone. I knew the floors were stone and that there were few rugs, that the windows were large and showed mountains, that the house was cold in winter. The cot was bound to be something of the sort, and a small child hears every sound with new ears, nothing shut off, as adults shut off sound. (UMS 20)

Above Lessing is creating autobiographic detail in the same way she writes a novel by transforming with an abundant use of fictional imaginationa little fragment of memoryand what she had heard from others (Lessing does not consider others' versions as significant) into a coherent narrative. The same method can be found in many places in *Under My Skin.*

Lessing explores various possibilities for evoking her past selves. For example, she awakes her past selves from her old photographs: "There survives a photograph of a thoughtful little girl, a credit to everyone concerned, but as it happens I remember what I was feeling ..." (UMS 38-39). Here Lessing attempts a detached narrative by addressing her own self as "a thoughtful little girl". "A credit to everyone concerned" is her present appreciation of the photograph. However, the way she recreatesher emotionhereis not drawn fromhermemory of her feelings, but isinduced when she watches the photograph objectively and interprets the child's emotions more closely.To Lessing, the old photographs, both of herself and her parents, are creative elements that can be used for self-discovery. She manipulates them constructively asarchaeological tools, along withher autobiographical imagination. Strikingly, she acknowledges them as her own younger selves she meets in her journey of self evolution.

Similarly, she usesimaginationcreatively when her memories fail. For example, she admits that she has only a frail memory of the long journey which she made from Persia to England with her parents.Instead of her partial and fragile memory (she rejects the authenticity and usefulness of such memories), which would fall shortof her parents'authentic accounts of the same, she creates a purely imaginative version of the same:

> A small girl sits on the train seat with her teddy and the tiny cardboard suitcase that has teddy's clothes in it. She takes the teddy's clothes off, folds them just so, takes another set of clothes from the case, dresses the teddy, tells it to be good and sit quietly, takes this set of clothes off the teddy, folds them.... (UMS 43)

Lessing's approach towards memory appears quite ambivalent in *Under My Skin.* On the one side, she expresses her disbelief in the authenticity of memories. She hesitates to accept all her memories as fact, since they cannot always be trusted. She exposes their unreliability by finding many of themasbiased and selective. She criticizes the unreliability of her memories during her train journey to England:

> Why ostriches, and not the ox wagons that still used the Salisbury streets, built wide so that the wagons could turn in them? Why the train in Russia but not the train Beira-to-Salisbury, surely equally exotic? Why remember this and not that? If I had decided to remember only the unpleasant, then why the ostriches, which were pure delight? (sic). (UMS 49)

Lessing says that "memory is a careless and lazy organ, not only a self-flattering one. And not always self-flattering"(UMS 13). She affirms that certain memories may not be factual, as there are fictional modes working within them. She directs this problem to her readers by saying thatthey can actually watch their minds doing it, taking a little fragment of fact, and spinning a tale out of it (UMS13). She also finds that certainmemories are not created by the subject (the person who remembers), but are imposed by his/her parents and addedlater. By evaluating the induced nature of many of her memories, Lessing reveals to her readers the errors lying in memories:

> A parent says, 'We took you to the seaside, and you built a sandcastle, don't you remember? Look, here is the photo'. And at once the child builds from the words and the photograph a memory, which becomes hers. (UMS13)

Lessing also blames memories forthe large gap they create between the time ofexperience and the time of recollection.Alarge gap lies between thechild's experience and the recollection of it when she becomes an adult. Lessing explains this as a crucial problemby citing examples from her own experience. There remain a lot of discrepancies between the child's time and the adult's time. She says how"a whole tract of time had disappeared" while "trying hard to make sense of my life through a strict use of memory" (UMS 59-60).

However, Lessing does not always hold a negative attitude towards memory.In spite of her distrust towards them, she still considers various ways oftriggering the memories of herearly childhood. In *Under My Skin* Lessing talks of her attempt to awake her childhood experiences by taking drugs (UMS 20-21). Similarly, she explores the stream-of-consciousness narrative forexploring and reconstructing her old and obscure memories:

> A TINY THING AMONG TRAMPLING, knocking careless giants who smell, who lean down towards you with great ugly hairy faces, showing big dirty teeth. A foot you keep an eye on, while trying to watch all the other dangers as well, is almost as big as you are ...(sic) (UMS 18)

Lessing's inclination towards fiction is evident from the very beginning of her autobiography. Although *Under My Skin* is subtitled "Volume One of My Autobiography to 1949", and a photo of Doris Lessing, aged fourteen, is placed in the inside front cover, adjacent to the title page, the initial chapter focuses more on Lessing's mother, Emily Maude Veagh Taylor, than on Lessing herself. The first chapter opens with a line of reported speech, not attributed to the speaker: "SHE WAS VERY PRETTY but all she cared about was horses and dancing"(sic) (UMS 1). From the next line the reader learns that the description is neither of the young girl in the photo, Lessing, nor of her mother, but rather her mother's mother.The line is a "refrain" which, shesays, "tinkled through my mother's tales of her childhood" (UMS 1). She begins her autobiography three generations before her own birth. The first chapter proceeds to describe Emily Maude's childhood and her life through her career as a nurse, her tragic romance with a ship's doctor, and her subsequent courtship and marriage with the wounded Alfred Taylor.

Lessing values her own imaginative portrayal, which she considers suitable to describe her grandmother. She negates the truth in the "refrain" which said "she was very pretty". She negates her mother'sdescriptionof her grandmother: "No, this is what she had heard from the servants, for she unconsciously put on a kitchen face, with a condemning look about her mouth, and she always gave a disapproving sniff"(UMS 1). At the end of the paragraph she gives a final picture of grandmother (opposed to what her mother made of her) saying that "Emily Flower was common, that must have been it" (1).

Lessing's portrayal of her grandparents (in *Under My Skin*) is not aimed to be exact; instead it reflects her therapeutic interest in analyzing her own parents' lives. She believes that parents would decide much of their children's emotional wakeups. For example, she sayshow her father's emotions influenced her:

> I think my father's rage at the trenches took me over, when I was very young, and has never left me. Do children feel their parents' emotions? Yes, we do, and it is a legacy I could have done without. What is the use of it? It is as if that old war is in my memory, my own consciousness". (AE257-58)

In *Under My Skin*Lessing prefers talking about her parents to talking about herself. She strongly reflects the view that she needs to explore much of her parents' lives to explore her own. The part of her autobiography that focuses on her parents looks more similar to a biography. She assumes and deduces information about her grandparents, and feels imagination as the apt medium in thisendeavour. Imagination provides her narrative freedom. She assumes of her grandmother's life:

> Emily came from this warm clan life into the doubtless ardent arms of John William McVeagh– he must have been very much in love to marry her–but she was expected to match herself to his ambitions, to the frightful snobberies of a man fighting to leave the working class behind. I imagine her running back home when she could to her common family, for dances, good times, and going to the races. She must have lived in her husband's house under a cold drizzle of disapproval, from which, or so I see it, she died, aged thirty two. (UMS 2)

By exploring deeply into her grandparents lives, Lessing deduces how their lives would have affectedher parents' lives. She also analyseshow her parents' personalitieswere distorted by their own parents. This is the way she interprets her parents' behaviour more healthily (she no more accuses her parents for the way they emotionally troubled her). Particularly, the gloomy picture Lessing creates of Emily, her grandmother,is fictional, but looks appropriate, because Lessing's readers encounter such confusion while analysing her mother's personality (both in *Under My Skin* and other autobiographical works). Moreover, Lessing believes that by closely analysing her grandparents she would be able to empathize with her mother better. A close observation of Lessing's portrait of her grandmother verifies that she isprojecting her own mother onto the unfamiliar figure of her grandmother.

Lessing also deduces that the distorted personality her mother developed would have been the effect of the nurture she had, particularly by "a typical step mother, cold, dutiful and correct, unable to be loving or even affectionate with the three children" (UMS 4). Shedescribes the unfavourable emotional nurture her parents received. Thus she assumes that the tragic (more emotional than physical) livesof her parents were the consequence of their up bringing (UMS 4).

The figures of her grandparents, which she constructs imaginatively, take her close to 'therapeutic truth'. Here the therapeutic truth remains opposed to the factual truth, i.e. the emotional suffering she had experienced from her parents and the resultant hatred she felt towards them. The truthprovides answers to many of thecomplex questions she has raised against her parents, foundat various points of her writing. She analytically interprets the shadowy figures of her grandparents by analysing the minds of her parents, andbyqueryinghow the former's emotions affected the latter. Imagination offers her the freedom to narrate and interpret the personalities of her grandparents and thereby interpret the lives of her parents. Consequently, after a long period of conflict and disagreement with her mother, Lessing recognizes her as a victim who was deprived of parental love and care. Later, readers watchhow she bestows her sympathies on her mother. This is a reconciliatory experience, which she experiences as therapeutic: "All you need is love. Love is all you need. A child should be governed by love, as mother so often said ..." (UMS 25).

Lessing narrates imaginative scenes of her mother'semotional suffering in front of her mother's strict and demanding father. Similarly shecompares her own experiencesthatare similar to her mother's, and tries to sympathize with her mother by seeing her as victim. Similarly, sheachieves a spurt of self-esteemby confirming that she can outlive the psychological hazards of such situations, unlike her mother who failed to outlive the situationsemotionally:

> She did not weep when her father was harsh: she stood up to him by being everything he demanded of her, and more. I on the other hand fought Marta for my rights in

that nursery, and unloved children are not 'nice', not 'gentle'. Who did love the child? Her father. The smell of maleness, tobacco, sweat, the smell of father, enveloped her in safety.(UMS28)

In *Under My Skin* we can see how Lessing learns to dream her formerly-divided self whole, primarily by imaginatively reconciling her lifelong conflict with her mother after her mother's death, and thereby offering a creative solution to her community of readers a possible way to heal a conflicted relationship that still tormented her, as evidenced by her preoccupation with mother-daughter conflicts in her fiction and autobiography. Forty years after her mother's death Lessing teaches herself to imaginatively reconcile her relationship with her mother, a reconciliation process which she begins with the first volume of autobiography and finally achieves in *Walking under the Shade*. She has acquired a new attitude towards her mother, which is more empathetic and forgiving than her earlier attitudes of rebellion, dislike and anger, which are apparent in her representations of the mother-daughter relationships in the earlier fictionalized versions.

Lessing resorts to imaginationfor constructingthe early lives of her parents, which is apparent in her later writings as well. For example, in her autobiographical project, *Alfred and Emily* (2008), she narrates the lives of her parentsimaginatively. In the first part of this work, *Alfred and Emily: a Novella*, sheuses fiction as an effective medium to explore the lives of her parents. By this fictional experiment she again emphasizes that much of her self-story is interlinked with her parents' life stories. She also emphasises that a more fictionalized autobiographicwork like *Alfred and Emily*is effective in the act of self-narration.

In *Alfred and Emily*, fiction is offering her the narrative freedom to explore her parents' lives. For example, in the first part of the work, she imagines freely how different her parents' lives would have been if there had been no world wars. In her introduction to*Alfred and Emily*, she states her intentionbehindfantasying (narrating the imagined) the lives of her parents: "I have tried to give them lives as might have been if there had been no World War One" (AE viii-viii). She says how she has fulfilled fictionally her father's desire to become a farmer without having enough money to buy a farm; and also how she has fulfilled her mother's desire to become the matron of the old Royal Free Hospital (AE viii-viii) (Lessing says she would surely have become the matron if she had not married Alfred). Here sheblends the imaginary and the real together for narrating her parents' lives, and within a sentence she tries to see the great difference that would have happened in their lives:

> Easy for my father.. He had wanted to be a farmer, all his life, in Essex or in Norfolk. He did not have money to buy a farm, so I have given him his heart's desire, which was to be an English farmer... Mymother... when she was thirty-two, she was offered the job of matron at St George's Hospital ... I used to joke, as a girl, that if she were in England she would be running the Women's Institute or like Florence Nightingale, be an inspiration for the reorganization of the hospitals. She was also musically talented.(AE viii-viii)

Certainly, in *Alfred and Emily*Lessing has a therapeutic purpose behind fictionalizing the story of her parents. She values the imaginative version of her parent's life as therapeutic, as it is a narrative of wish fulfilment. In fact, in *Alfred and Emily*Lessing states this purpose (AE viii).

A close analysisof *Alfred and Emily*reveals that, by apparently fictionalizing the lives of her parents, she is nottrying to mystify her familiar reading community; instead, she is suggesting them a means of emotional healing through self-writing.While narrating the imaginary lives of her parents, Lessing is boldly constructing an alternative version of reality; she dares not do the same in her early writings, where her fictional attempts aremore subtle. In *Alfred and Emily*, she gives expression to her parents' and her own inner longings, hopes, dreams, ambitions and aspirations that are generally subtle, demanding close analysis. She says that in writing about her father's imagined life andthat of her mother's, she has"relied not only traits of character that may be extrapolated, or extended, but on tones of voice, sighs, wistful looks, signs as slight, as those used by skilful trackers" (A E 139).

In Lessing's quest of self, imagination does the work of a dream, since she considers both dream and imagination as modes of wish-fulfilment. For example, just likeshe constructsthe imaginative lives of her parents in *Alfred and Emily*, she constructsfor her an'imaginative rebirth'in *Under My Skin*. She calls it a happy "rebirth" and "a therapeutic good birth" that she has constructed through fiction (UMS 21).

Often, she finds interest in creating whimsical versions of her life-events. For example, in *Alfred and Emily*, particularly in the first part of it, readerswatch how she constructs a whimsical version of her parents' lives, which is far removed from the factual traumatic one. Here she is exploring the therapeutic power of imagination, by contrasting the imaginary with the real. Through imaginary narration, she thinks that she can compensate for what she had missed in reality. In fact, *Alfred and Emily*, which she has suggested as her final work, is animaginary fulfilment of her constant longing. She has remarked about that longing in *Under My Skin*:

> I once thought of writing a book called My Alternative Lives ... But the plot here would be ... set in other parallel universes or 'realities', continually influencing mine. A nice idea for a book, but time is running out. (UMS 228)

It is clear from Lessing's words above that she manipulates imagination, like dreams, as a mode of wish fulfilment in her act of self narration. Thus, she does not see much difference between the factual world and the dream world. There is only a flimsy boarder existing between the two in her works.

Next, Lessing's writing is characteristically noted for her characters' multiple selves and multiple dialogues, and *Under My Skin* andAlfred *and Emily* are no exception to this case. Hazel Markus and Paula Nuriousin their collaborated work "Possible Selves"demonstrate the pattern of self-recovery, which the individual undergoes in narrative therapy (22-68). Lessing's strategy in dealing with the multiple selves in *Under My Skin* and *Alfred and Emily* functions close to that of Markus's and Nurious'.

Themultiple selvesshe fictionally creates in the two works aremore 'possible selves', and her attempt at creating them can be convincingly suggested as her struggle for creating a new identity.Thus,as Lessing constructs new identities of her parents in *Alfred and Emily*,she subtly creates for her a new identity in *Under My Skin*.It is achieved by giving shape to those past selves that ever remained within her as 'possible-selves', which she tries to realise now,whichis also an act of self realisation. However,of the two works, the intentionis clearerin *Alfred and Emily*than in *Under My Skin*,wherethe attemptmore subtle.

While she is probing and analyzing the'multiple selves'and 'possible selves'within her, she strives to project in front of the public 'a more desirable self'. Among her desirable past selves in *Under My Skin*, "Tigger" is strikingly noticeable. This personality appears in several places. However, by the name "Tigger", Lessing is not representinga single personality, but many. They include "the fat and bouncy Tigger", "Tigger Tayler", "Tigger Wisdom", "Tigger Lessing", and "Comrade Tigger" (UMS 89-90).Lessing's projecting Tigger's personality intermittently in *Under My Skin* has been commented on as her use of double personas in the work (Wittacker123-24).

Lessing also operates a 'divided self' or a 'split self' throughout *Under My Skin*, which can alsobe connectedto her strategy of self-analysis. She tries to divide her into two distinct personalities, which shecallsthe "private self" and the "public self", without revealing to the public that the private self is acting as the 'observer' within:

> But behind all that friendly helpfulness was something else, the observer and it is here I retreat to, take refuge, when I think that my life will be a public property and there is nothing I can do about it. You will never access here, you can't, this is the ultimate and inviolable privacy... (UMS 20)

On the other hand, Lessing identifies the "public self", the "hostess personality", which acts as a protection to the "private self":

> What I learned then was how strong in me was the personality I call the Hostess, for I was presenting my experience to them, chatting away increasingly scatty, but in control, but all that was a protection for what went on within. This Hostess personality, bright, helpful, attentive, receptive to what is expected, is very strong indeed. It is a protection, a shield, for the private self. (UMS 20)

Dramatic narrative shifts can also be notedin various places of *Under My Skin*. Lessingoccasionally shifts the narrative position from the first person to the third.She also shifts the narrative mode from the subjectiveto the objective, and shifts the direction of analysis from the outside to inside and vice versa. Here she is trying for a narrative distance, so that the observer within her may get a more objective and close view ofthe other personalities in her. This narrative technique enables her to observe herself with a detached curiosity, as if she were the other (UMS 12).Sheaddresses her *selves*in the third person pronouns and by using different names that may appear as the author's playfulness at the beginning, which later gets confirmed as a strategized positioning. The same artin self-writing is also suggested by Pennebaker as a therapeutic strategy. He observes that, by adopting this strategized positioning, the self-narrator can imitate the analyst-analysand patterning in psychotherapy (*Telling Stories* 3-18). In that way, ifLessing is mediating this positionshe is playing the role of the analyst.

Lessing convincingly explains this detached positioning as her own strategy intendedfor self-analysis:

> Now I look back that child, that girl, that young woman, with a more and more detached curiosity. Old people may be observed peering into their pasts. Why?– they are asking themselves. How did that happen? I try to see my past selves as someone else might, and then put myself back inside one of them, and am at once submerged in a hot struggle of emotion, justified by thoughts and ideas I now judge wrong. (UMS 12)

The private self, whom Lessing calls the 'observer', is the analyst. It is not only acting as the observer, but also as the healer. For example, Lessing says how she (the observer) searches, fixes, consoles and heals one of her selves:

> The other person, or personality, was a sobbing child. I wept and wept, much to the concern of my companions, but I know it was not important, my weeping. I do not cry enough; that has always been true, and to weep without constraint was a bonus and bliss. I could easily have cradled that poor baby and comforted her...(UMS 21)

By calling "the other person", "a sobbing child", and "that poor baby", Lessing's observer is fixing one of her distinct childhood selves, which still require healing. In the next paragraph of the same page she reveals the complexity (instead of the easiness she initially felt) of such an attempt, as she sees the number of such childhood selves (the selves that require healing)are multiplying (21).Thus, the strong therapeutic interests emphasised by Lessing is a strong evidence forherpersonal standagainst the confessional mode usually expected from autobiography.

4

Self-Writing and Self-Healing in Fiction

Even as Lessing strategizes her autobiographical writings for her own self-quest and self-healing, she constructs many of her novels as her protagonists' search into their selves and self-healing. Critics agree that Lessing's protagonists resemble her in many ways (Maslen 28). For example, Martha Quest, Lessing's protagonist in her *Children of Violence* series, resembles the young Doris Lessing who grew up in the farms. Lessing also admits that her own younger personality as portrayed in Martha Quest (A E 178).

Another characteristic of Lessing's protagonists is that, just like Lessing does in her autobiographical works, they engage in the act of self-analysis and self-quest. They also engage in autobiographical enquiries into their self and selfhood. The way Lessing focusesonher protagonist's self-quest cannot be neglected; rather, it is to be closely linked with her own therapeutic enquiry through fiction.

Lessing engages with the possibility of non-rational and non-logical modes of knowledge that enables an individual to perceiveher inner self and construct an inner dialogue within her. Her conception of the human psyche is contrary to conventional concepts,and she tries to evolve her own perception about it. Her protagonists experience emotional and psychological trauma. They also experience severe identity crises, which may bea sign of impendingpsychological breakdown. However, Lessing sees her characters' breakdown as a channel for them to see their inner problems, which also provides them an insight into the need for achieving self-healing. Her approach towards mental disorder proves that she is in favour of the anti-psychiatricconcepts that question the conventional approaches of psychiatrythat stigmatizes individuals under the names of different mental disorders. For example, in her novel *Briefing aDescent to Hell*, she reflects her belief that one's experience in madness could be far more expressive than his/her normal experiences. Similarly, the surrealistic perception that her characters achieve is far more self-reflective than other modes perception. In *Briefing a Descent to Hell*, she describes the strange experience of the protagonist, Charles Watkins, whose descent into deep madness in turn becomes a self-revelatory experience to him.

Similarly, shetreats'self-healing' as a significant theme in almost all her writings. This emphasises herconvictionabout the individual's innate ability toachieve self-healing. Just like the physical mechanism of healing, the self has an inherentability to heal itself. Many critics suggest that her belief in self-healing is similar to that of the 'individuation' process, as suggested by Carl Jung (Wittaker 11).Jung, who introduced this concept, points out that like a living bodythe human mind also has an innate ability to heal itself. He holds that just like thephysical ailments thatare external signs of the body's effort to regain health, psychological disorders are the external signs of the mind's effort to self-heal (Storr 80-93). In most of her novels Lessing presents her protagonists acting as their own healers. Similar to her experience in her autobiographical writings, in her fictional works she creates her protagonists who on behalf of her continue her journey of self-enquiry and self-healing.

Lessing acknowledges her characters' freedom to go deep into their subjectivity and to analyze the condition of their inner selves. Unconventional in fictional writings, Lessing chooses the first person narrative in certain places that give her protagonists a sense of freedom to enter themselves, and their subjectivity. Numerous examples can be cited in her fictional workswhere her protagonists engage in self-reflective intrapersonal interactions within themselves, similar to that which the autobiographical narrative permits. Often, Lessing intermittently describes her protagonists' exploration into their own dreams. They enjoy a sense of freedom to enter their dreams and analyze themselves at will. This freedom is again similar to that which she enjoys in her autobiographical writings.

The focus here is on analyzing how Lessing's protagonists, namely, Anna Wulf in *The Golden Notebook* and Kate Brown in *The Summer Before the Dark* (sic),experience identity crises and psychological breakdown in the beginning, and later, how they act as self-analysts and self-healers. The concept of 'self as narrative' is still relevant and illuminative here.We can compare Lessing's own act of self narration and self-analysis in her autobiographical writings and her creation of protagonists who act as their own self healers. Lessing's concern for her protagonists' self-quest is interesting; the verification of it would substantiate the therapeutic strategies she has applied in her self-representational writings. In addition to this, Lessing's consideration of her characters as their own healers would emphasise her belief of the individual's capacity to achievepsychological integration and wholeness.

Besides the intrapersonal reflections carried on within the protagonists' minds, Lessing is keen on observing and projecting interpersonal relationships. In fictional writings, particularly in *The Golden Notebook* and *The Summer before the Dark* (sic), Lessing discovers the significance of interpersonal relationships in constructing one's self. Interpersonal relationships can become self-constructive or self-destructive. She is keen on analyzing her characters' interpersonal relationships and how these move towards self-disintegration or self-healing.

The central theme of *The Golden Notebook* and *The Summer before the Dark* (sic) is the same. Both works describe the identity crises that Lessing's protagonists experience in certain stages of their lives. There are a number of similarities between Anna Wulf and Kate Brown. Both of them reflect the intelligent and assertive spirit of Lessing. Similarly, both of them are passing or about to pass the emotionally turbulent middleage, a critical juncture in the lives of almost all her characters.

Anna Wulf is a successful, ex-communist writer, who lives alone with her daughter Janet. She is divorced and has freed herself from the bondage of domesticity. The novel pictures how Anna's friendship with Molly, an ex-communist actor, mirrors a lot of similarities between them. Their mutual relationship as'free women'later develops as a significant motif in the novel.

Likewise, in *The Summer before the Dark* (sic), Kate Brown, the protagonist, liberates herself from the bondage of domesticity after twenty years of being a good wife and mother. Her husband, Michael, is occupied with his own job, while her four grown up children like to enjoy their lives independently of their mother. The novel describes Kate's identity crisis as caused by her emotional disruptions within the family, and then, her quest for self-fulfilment and self revelatory experience that aresymbolized in her spiritual and real life journey. After forty years of submissive confinement inside the prison of the family, she leaves her husband and children to take up her new job as a translator at Global Food in Istanbul. This journey,with itsnumerous mythical and spiritual implications, symbolizes her quest for a new identity.

Lessing's choiceof the non-rational path towards self-knowledge can be located in *The Summer before the Dark* (sic). Often, her protagonists are gifted with non-rational insights, by which they indulge in self-reflective intrapersonal interactions at will. Their experience can be compared to self-analysis through self-writing, which Lessing finds deeply insightful and thereby therapeutic in her autobiographies. At the beginning of the novel, Kate Brown receives a deeper insight of her inner breakdown, which she recognizes as the consequence of her middleage crisis (SBD 9-10).

Kate compares herself with Mary Fincherly, andis shocked to recognize that Mary owns a higher self-worth than herself. Kate has not felt the same before. Shealways saw herself in a better light while comparing her with Mary, whom she considered immoral andtreacherous. However, instead of her higher self-worth at present, Kate experiences recurring feelings of regression and self worthlessness. Nowshe acknowledges that she was negating her identity for her family, where she lacks any significant role now.

Kate feels quite inferior and plain in her appearance, as "she did not allow her appearance to bloom, because she had observed early in the children's adolescence how much they disliked her giving rein her own nature" (SBD 11).She feels herselfworthless in comparison with Mary Fincherly, who,in contrast to Kate,"dressed as she would have done if she had no children and was unmarried" (SBD 11).

Kate's emotional breakdown reflects not only her middle age crisis, but also the mother-child conflict, a significant theme which Lessing takes up in almost all her writings. Kate sees herself as the symbol of a middle-aged mother, who sacrificed both her freedom and prospects for her children. She compares her condition to that of a stray cat, which she is looking after now. By empathising with the catshe foregrounds her bitter solitude, which is also an expression of self-pity (SBD 96). She feels that her children's attitude towards the cat is a reflection of their feelings towards Kate: "Oh, go on, you've taken in that smelly old cat just because we aren't being nice to you!"(96).

Unlike her typical treatment of the mother-daughter relationship in her other writings, in *Summer Before the Dark* Lessing analyzes the emotional struggles of a middle-aged mother againsther grownup children. For example, sheanalyzes the emotional outburst of the middle-aged mother against her young, self-centred children: "Now she wished that she had slapped hard her delightful daughter Eileen, her charming Michael, Tim– all of them. 'I wish I had hit him', she heard herself mutter; 'I do, I had hit them all hard!'"(SBD 96). On the other hand, particularly in her autobiographical writings, Lessing tries to watch the subjective emotions of the daughter against her mother. This can be found at many places in *Under My Skin*, where Lessing expresses the emotional outburst of the daughter against her mother.

Another reason for Kate's identity crisis is motherhood. Lessing's perspective changes from time to time. It is clear that her perspective of human life has progressed in the course of time. Lessing, who has sympathized with adolescent daughters who suffer emotionally and psychologically under their possessive mothers, now tries to watchthe other side of life (SBD 94-98). She watches the middle-aged mother, who has sacrificed her whole life for her children, gets deeply wounded: "'just the thing of menopause', she had heard Tim say to Eileen. She had not started the menopause, but it would have been no use of saying so: it had been useful, apparently, for the family's mythology to have a mother in the menopause" (96-97). Through the story of Kate, Lessing tries to look inside the darker sides of motherhood.

From another point of view, Kate's identity crisis can be seen as a consequence of the breakdown in interpersonal relationships. A person's identity is constructed in intimate relationships, and the breakdown of such relationships would surely affect his/her sense of identity. For the long twenty five years of her life she was dutifulsolely to her family. Her intimate relationships were confined to her family. At this period of crisis she regrets how foolishly she had sacrificed her freedom and identity,in her devotion to her husband and children. Instead of her earlier devotion to the family, she feels that domesticity isbondage.

Her *self* has suffered much in her interpersonal relationships with her family. In *The Summer Before the Dark* (sic) she analyzes how interpersonal relationships, particularly family bonds, can act as a self-destructive force. As for Kate, continuing her life within her family is equal to sacrificing her self-identity.

Kate's story can be considered as her search for self-healing, but Lessing's treatment of the novel does not support the view that the story has feminist undertones. For example, the novel ends with Kate's decision to come back to her home to spendher time again with her husband and children.The novel impliesin clearterms that Kate's leaving her family can be taken as a part of her quest for identity, which leads her towards self-healing.

In *The Golden Notebook* Anna's problem is very similar to that of Kate in *The Summer Before the Dark* (sic). Like Kate Brown, the cause of Anna's breakdown is her identity crisis. Anna experiences an inner breakdown, which appearsclose to a schizophrenic episode.In her preface to the work, Lessing announces that the central theme of the novel is 'breakdown' (GN xii). The same is also projected symbolically through the structure and language of the novel. *The Golden Notebook* is a compilation of various texts, which consists five notebooks and an embedded novella, 'Free Women'. Written in imitation of conventional narrative,'Free Women'is divided into five parts. Except the fifth chapter every segment of the 'Free Women' is tagged with the fragment of four notebooks. The colours of the notebooks distinguish different facets of Anna's life, and they arestructured in the order of black, red, yellow, and blue. 'The Black Notebook' focuses on Anna the writer, and her memory of her early experiences in Africa; the 'Red Notebook' deals with her political activities; the 'Yellow Notebook' is a fictionalized account of her sexual relations; and the 'Blue Notebook' is a diary. At the end of the last sequence of notebooks, Anna uses a new 'Golden Notebook', which records her experiences during her descent into madness. The fifth segment of "Free Women" puts a period after the mass of the five notebooks. "Free Women" can be seen as a summary of Anna's experiences that are discursively documented in the five notebooks.

Since the beginning of the novel, Anna faces the problem of self-definition. Anna's identity crisis can be attributed to her inability to define her *self*. The compartmentalized structure of the novel symbolizes Anna's desperate struggle to integrate her multiple selves. Anna has to act various roles in life that includeher roles as mother, wife, friend, lover, and an active communist. By telling the story of Anna, Lessing emphasises her affinity towards the narrative concepts of self – i.e. a person conceivesher *self* in a storied form,which is conceptualized through the act of narration. The act of self narration enables the person to construct a coherent, integrated and meaningful version of her life. In her preface to *The Golden Notebook*Lessing asserts how"the essence of the book, the organization of it, everything in it, says implicitly and explicitly, that we must not divide things off, must not compartmentalise" (GN xv). Thus, throughthe story of Anna, Lessing analyze show the conflicting roles that Anna plays lead herinto self-fragmentation,and in turn towards self-destruction.

Anna's identity crisis deteriorates with her dependence on others for defining her *self*. By surrendering her will to others,she is sacrificing her authority and freedom to define her individual *self*. Anna occasionally uses the term 'free women' and tries to identify with it. However, this attempt is quite paradoxical, sincemost of her relationships – those she hadin the past and experiencing in the present, the imaginary and the real – act like bondages, which takeaway her individual freedom from defining her real *self*. Anna's schizophrenia is aneffect of her passive agreement to surrender her will to others. Thus, Anna's inability to define her *self* causes her identity crisis, which in turnleads her to a state of complete breakdown.

Of all the notebooks, the 'Red Notebook' best exemplifies people's desire to join a group because they are attracted to social fantasy. Anna's involvement withCommunism and her relationship with her Communist colleagues are among the main reasons for her intensified identity crisis and schizophrenia. In fact, she joins the Communist party in order to gain a sense of integration, hoping that this will prevent her from further breakdown. However, staying in the party only accelerates her breakdown. She observes that the Communist party is fabricated by a false myth in which the principle of self-division is inherent. She realizes that the existence of theCommunist party lies in the members' agreement with the self-dividing principle of the party at any given moment (GN 64). Like Molly, Anna joins the party in spite of herself. They join the party just to prove that they are truly practising their Communist ideals.

After joining the party, Anna is critical of it. The Communists are immersed in ideology, which is intended to constitute the party to such an extent that they assume their roles as Communists at the expense of their real selves. Therefore, Anna observes two personalities evolving from the same person. When discussing political issues in the party, aCommunist talks as if he owns a second personality. On the one hand, he sticks to the Communist myth. On the other, he is fully aware of the enormous gap between the ideal and the reality. Anna observes the split lurking in the same communist when he publicly asserts that only Communism can improve the world, while in his mind he doubts its possibility (GN153).

Anna recognizes her own split personalityby observing her self-deceiving tone, like that used by other Communists. During her talk with molly, Anna notices the conflict between her two personalities. However, she fails to control them. She notices "the dry, wise, ironical, political woman or the party fanatic who sounds literally quite maniacal"(GN 153). Anna's stammer is also an indication of the conflict between her split personalities. By listening to the Communist's tone of self-deception, Anna realizes the cause of her stammer. She listens tothe Communist's tone, which is "the simple, bluff, I-am-a-good-fellow tone which I use myself sometimes" (Sic)(GN 286). Her stammer gets worsened with her lecture to the Communists on the subject of art, which is the product of group consciousness and not that of the individual egotism. On the surface, Communism encourages its members to give up their egotism for the sake of the community (GN 334).

However, Anna cannot quench her desire for individual art, which actually clashes with the Communist concept of art. Seeing that joining the party only makes her more isolated and split, she decides to leave it forever (GN 154). On her way back home after her intellectual conflict with Communism, she evaluates how she resorted tothe party for wholeness and to save herself from "the split, divided, unsatisfactory way we all live"(GN 154). To her disappointment, she also realizes that the essence of Communism is alienation. She saysit is "alienation. Being split. It's the moral side, so to speak, of the Communist message" (sic) (GN 344).

Another element which can be attributed to Anna's identity crisis and her mental breakdown is her willingness to involve in self-destructive interpersonal relationships.Marriage, which Anna expects to betheway forself-protection, in turn becomes a cage in which she is trapped emotionally, forever. In the Black Notebook, Anna sees how her marriage with Michael bound her inside the cage of domesticity. Similarly, she watches her own condition through Molly and Marion, who are the other victims of marriage. She continues to examine her own experience through watching other women's experience. Women succumb to their husbands'insistence on defining their selves. The roles women and men playare that of victims and persecutors. Women are contentto act the role of victims by surrendering their freedom to their husbands. This chain of relationship continues for years. It is difficult for women to extricate themselves from the fantasy of marriage because they are perplexed by the guilt feeling from the resentment against inequality between men and women.

In addition to the man-woman bondagewithin marriage,such relationship outside marriage too can be bondage. In *The Golden Notebook*, Anna's identity crisis is the consequence of such relationships also. For example, Anna's insight into her intimate relationships with men provides her a new understanding of love and sexuality. In the 'Yellow Notebook' she comes to realize that the theme of the novel, 'The Shadow of the Third' implies the naiveté embedded in the concept of love.There Ellaappears as the alter ego of Anna. Through the relationship between Ella and Paul Anna analyses her own relationship with Michael. It is Ella's naiveté that blocks her from perceiving the reality of Paul'sintimacy with her, and it is derived from her willingness to let Paul destroy her intelligence.He destroys the "knowing, doubting, sophisticated Ella and again and againhe put her intelligence to sleep, and with her willing connivance, so that she floated darkly on her love for him ...(GN 200-01).

Ella's creative faith in Paul makes her intellectually blind, and thereby she becomes willing to surrender her*self*to Paul's will. Although Ella knows that Paul is breaking away from her, she is unable to give up her hope that Paul would continue to visit her. She stupidly expects Paul to divorce his wife to marry her. Ella's expectation of impractical happiness is the real cause of her naiveté, which makes her surrender her will to Paul.

Anna gets emotionallydisturbed while watching the destructive power in interpersonal relationships, particularly man-woman relationships. She observesthat those relationships are grounded on the preservation of egotism, and therefore, in such relationships a person is not concerned with the wellbeing of the other individual with whom he/she establishes the relationship. Thus self-protection has been deemed as the priority of the survival.

Anna experiences the cannibal/victim patterning in men-women relationships. Men play the role of cannibal while women choose the role of victim. The cannibal invades the victim's freedom and deprives her of her will. However, men cannot merely take the role of the cannibal unless women surrender their will to act as victims. Anna recognises thatthe victims are "those who've given up being cannibals themselves; they're not tough or ruthless enough for the golden road to maturity and the ever-so-wise shrug"(GN544). The cannibal requires the victim's self-sacrifice on which he can build up his path to maturity,as the cannibal preserves his identity and subjectivity by depriving the victim of her will and freedom.

Similarly, since the very beginning of the novel, Anna tends to efface her identity in her interpersonal relationships. Moreover, her self-effacement is deliberate. Thus, this emphasises that Anna's identity crisis is due to her inability to keep her sense of self identity intact. Anna experiences her interpersonal relationships as a threat to her identity. She experiences a sort of self-effacement in almost all her interpersonal relationships. This can be convincingly verified since the beginning of *The Golden Notebook*. On the one side, Anna suffers from the self-destructive elements that she observes and experiences in men-women relationships; and on the other side,she experiences some sort of engulfment which intensifies her identity crisis and schizophrenia.

Although she experiences severe vulnerability in relationships, she is unable to protect her subjectivity from others. She is not only disturbed of what happens in her life; she is equally disturbed of what happened to others, as though it happened to her. This empathetic tendency gets worsened, and she experiences it attacking her sense of subjectivity. For example, in "Free Women", the readers see that the beginning of Anna's problem is the consequence of her entanglement with the family disputes of Molly.It seems that certain similarities between the two made them close friends. Anna andMolly share several similarities. Both were Communists once; and now both have rejected their faith. Similarly, they have divorced their husbands; and now they are living alone with their children. Anna fancies much of their common experience, which is quite evident in her dialogues with Molly (GN 51).

As mentioned before, Anna's emotional disturbance is a result of her interference with the family disputes of Molly, particularly Molly's problem with her ex-husband, Richard, and her son Tommy. Moreover, unable to hurt her intimate friend, Anna willingly sacrifies her individual identity in her relationship with Molly.Evidently, she experiences a sort of self effacement in her relationship with Molly, and she willingly allows herself to be effaced when she is with Molly (GN 9).

In their relationship Anna deliberatelyacts the role of a submissive daughter who allows herto be emotionally dominated by the mother figure, Molly. Anna transfers her mother's image onto Molly, and begins fighting desperately to get herself free from the domineering mother's image in Molly (GN 40,430). Anna's unwillingness to change her submissive role is due to her fear of breaking her relationship with Molly. However, due to her willingness to comply with this role, she pays the price – her gradual loss of self and identity. Anna's self-effacement begins with this relationship, and continues throughout the novel. Tonya Krousecomments of this that throughout "Free Women" as well as in the individual notebooks, readers repeatedly witness Anna rendered faceless on the page, not only in relation to Molly, but also in relation to other characters that populate the text (43-44). Molly's dominance over Anna and Anna's willing submissiveness are fictionally analyzed in the Yellow Notebook also. Ella's attachment with Julia in the Yellow Notebook is Anna's fictional analysis of her relationship Molly (GN430).

The self-destructive nature of Anna's interpersonal relationships can also be observed in Anna's relationship with her daughter Janet. Anna's self-disintegration is also caused by the self-fragmentation which she creates while playing the role of a mother. She fails to integrate her roles as Janet's mother and Michael's mistress. She willingly accepts these two roles that contradict each other, which further fragments her sense of identity: "And I prefer it, because it divides me. The two personalities–Janet's mother, Michael's mistress, are happier separated. It is a strain having to be both at once" (GN 321). It was also her false belief that her existence is only significant for her role as Janet's mother and that her identity as Janet's mother would protect her from total breakdown(GN 373). Later, sheis forced to revise her belief (GN 551,565).

Her interpersonal entanglement becomes so apparentwith her gradual loss of subjectivity, due to her act of self-effacement. It is essential for a person to have a firm sense of identity so that she/he can establish a healthy relationship with another person. Her anxiety of losingher subjectivity originates from her inability to conceive an autonomous identity. A person's lack of continuous and autonomous identity puts him/her under constant threat of vulnerability in interpersonal relationships. Likewise, shefeels threatened by others whom she thinks would attack her sense of subjectivity. For example, when she gets off a train, she feels intimidated by the approach of a stranger who intends to chat with her. She gets panicky, and cries frantically to him to go away. She analyses her experience later and thinks why she had felt so. She realizes that this is a usual event, but the emotion she had felt then was quite unusual to her (GN 374).

Both *The Golden Notebook* and *The Summer Before the Dark* (sic) have been appreciated by many readersfor their feminist undertones (Krouse 41-43). On the one side, Lessing's protagonists suffer identity crises and resulting mental breakdown; on the other, her protagonists viewthese as a meansto achieve self-recovery. Kate and Anna experience their identity crises as way to discover their inner selves. It is this that provides them an insight into the fragmented nature of their inner selves, which otherwise they would not have realized with their 'sane' state of mind.

From this perspective, Lessing's approach towards various mental disorders looks close to that of the outlook of the anti-psychiatry movement, which called for discarding the traditional approach to psychological disorders. Lessing's view emphasises that individuals' experience during mental disorders can be far more constructive to their inner selves, which enable them to move towards their self- healing. Thus, the two novels are substantial evidences of Lessing's slant towards anti-psychiatric concepts, particularly the concept of the individual's innate ability to achieve self-recovery.

Thus, Lessing's description of her protagonists' identity crisis, the resulting mental breakdown, and their self-healing experience resemble her own experiences which she wields through her autobiographical writing. Both Anna's and Kate's recoveries progress in a similar pattern, and it involves the same therapeutic strategies that Lessing has employed. Among them, the most significant is the analyst-analysand patterning, which Lessing hasalso explored in her autobiographical writings.

It is Lessing's narrative style that makes the analyst-analysand patterning possible in fiction as well. Her characteristic style in fictional writing enables her to explore her protagonists' subjectivity which would make this strategy possible. Thus, Lessing's narrative act of self-analysis in her autobiography has successfully been carried out by her protagonists.

Lessing's interest in exploring her character's subjectivity is evident in her great interest in probing into their dreams. Similarly, herprotagonists see their dreams as self-reflective experiences. Often, dreams enable them tokeep an inner dialogue withinthemselves.They also realize their inner struggles by using the medium of dreams. The world of dreams opens to them the world of intuitive knowledge,which enables to see their inner selves, which is far superior to the rational path towards self-knowledge. They often discern the fantastic, mythical, archetypal, and symbolic dimensions of their dreams, and what these elements signify to their selves. The significance which Lessing's protagonists attribute to their dreams is clear. For example, in *The Summer Before the Dark* (sic), Kate realizes the significance of her dreams, and what they are able to communicate to her (SBD 124-125).

In her ongoing dreams Kate embarks ona mythical journey with a wounded seal, which she finds half dead; her attempt to revitalize it with sea water finally succeeds. In fact, she realizes the significance of her ongoing dream, and what the seal has to tell of the state of her inner self. Kate, like Lessing's other protagonists, experiences the act of dreaming as an act of dialogue that takes place within her. Moreover, the dream journey with the seal acts as a parallel and corresponding experience to the ongoing physical journey, which is described within the 'realistic' part of the story. Kate could enter and re-enter her dream at will:

> But this dream, the dream of the seal, was of a different quality from any she had known. Not because it seemed so 'real' – many of her dreams did, as real as waking life. No, it was because of its atmosphere, so particularly its own that she could enter into it even when the seal was not there … She could enter the place of the dream and know it to be the dream of the seal. Going to sleep and entering this dream was as much as her business for this time…. (SBD 125)

Anna's self-discovery in *The Golden Notebook* too is partly indebted to her attemptto interpret her dreams. Her dreams act the role of a guide in her effort for self-discovery. Anna's dreams, like Kate's, are mythical:

> Anna slept and dreamed. She was standing on the edge of a wide yellow desert at midday. The sun was darkened by the dust hanging in the air. The sun was a baleful orange colour over the yellow dusty expanse. Anna knew she had to cross the desert. Over it, on the far side, were mountains – purple and orange and gray … (GN 390-391)

Anna suffers severe mental breakdown and identity crisis when she is confused about what to do with Ronnie and Ivor. On the one side, she wants both Ronnie and Ivor to get out her house, as she believes that letting the homosexuals stay inside her house would obliterate her sense of identity as a heterosexual. At the same time, she lacks the will to say them that they should leave her flat. It is the dream that she watches brings back her will, and thereby shefinds her way towards self-recovery (GN 391).

In her fictional writings Lessing focuses on her protagonists' ability to create intrapersonal dialogues, and on how nonconventional ways of communication can help them to solve their inner conflicts and achieve self-healing. Lessing's writing throws asearchlighton her protagonists' distant dream voyages that are always set in their inner worlds. In fact through her protagonists Lessing emphasizes that the act of dreaming is an act of self-analysis, and the intrapersonal communication which they establish through dreaming creates an analyst-analysand pattern.

Lessing's characters search alternative ways for self-analysis, and they see dreams as just one of the ways for achievingself recovery. For example, in *The Golden Notebook* Anna's act of self-writing can be seen as a therapeutic act of self-analysis. Anna's attempt to keep four notebooks at once represents her intention ofdividing and fixing her various selves. In the *Golden Notebook*, Anna's un-embodied self watches her body from outside: "She saw herself, Anna, seated on the music-stool, writing, writing; divided, bracketed, broken... turning the pages of her orderly notebooks" (373). Similarly, while writing the notebooks, she observes herself watching her conflicting, divided selves. She looks at her notebooks just "as if she were a general on the top of the mountain watching her armies deploy in the valley below" (68). This unembodied self serves as an onlooker, observing from outside what the body is experiencing. Attempting to reintegrate her life, Anna realizes that the fiction she creates serves as a mirror, reflecting her fragmented consciousness (68).

Anna's decision to keep the four notebooks takes her further into her subjectivity through the act of self-analysis. At first she resorts to the freedom and the objectivity that fiction offers her in the act of self-analysis. Anna's dependence on fiction for self-analysis reflects her belief that writing should be impersonal. Through the Yellow Notebook Anna writes her novel "The Shadow of the Third", andthere she tries to watch herself objectively through the fictional character, Ella.

Ella is Anna's alter ego, and by writing the fictional story of Ella, Anna is able to construct an inner dialogue within her. By creating her alter ego in the fictional character Ella, Anna experiences a sort of self-effacement, which is partially responsible for the obliteration of her subjectivity. Anna's intention of creating Ella can be explained as her need to create an observing Anna, to look at her life from an objective perspective. Again the act of writing i.e., Anna's writing 'The Shadow of the Third' about Ella, along with Ella's writing a novel about herself, demonstrates the Anna's attempt to createthe multiple representation of her own*self*.

However, Anna continuously encounters the threat of self-erasure, and even her resorting to fiction for self-analysis does not promiseher the protection of self-identity. For example, she continuously experiences self-erasure even in her attempt to create her alter ego through the fictional character Ella. Krause finds that the writer Anna herself is responsible for the obliteration of her subjectivity, and adds that Anna's fictional writing enacts and re-enacts her act of self-effacement:

> As the Annas of the text write themselves into being, they also engage in repeated cancellation of the self through writing. In fact ...they seem to do so in order to facilitate subsequent self-cancellation or self-erasure. (Krouse 42)

Anna's writing of Ella, and her intention of self-analysis through Ella reveals Anna's attempt to hide herself from others: "They would still be anonymous— that was the quality, anonymity. The safety of the anonymity" (GN 465).

In the later part the novel, Anna realizes that the fictional strategy in self-representation does not meet with her intention of self-analysis:

> It struck me that my doing this– turning everything into fiction– must be an evasion. Why not write down, simply, what happened between Molly and her son today? Why do I never write down, simply, what happens? Why don't I keep a diary? Obviously, my changing everything into fiction is simply a means of concealing something from myself". (GN 217)

It is Anna's realization that her choice of fiction is in fact her fear of meeting with reality. Anna's denial of fiction and her choosing of the dairy reflect the change in her belief that writing should be impersonal. By choosing the diary to narrate her *self*, Annacrosses the boundary between writing and living. Her attempt to keep diaries reflects her individual attempt to integrate her divergent experiences. Particularly, it would be interesting to watch how Anna crosses the boundaries of sleep and wakefulness in her diaries by assimilatingher experienceswith dream and reality.

Thus, in addition to fiction-writing, diary writing also signifies Anna's efforts to create self-interaction, and thereby self-integration. Similarly, Anna's diary writing emphasises her individual attempt to narrate her self-story and thereby preserve her self-identity. Diary writing is a reaction on the part of Anna, who is continuously experiencing self-erasure in spite her effort to cohere her conflicting sense of identity. By keeping a diary, Anna thinks she is able to integrate her various life events, which otherwise would remain disintegrated and fragmented. She realizes that diary writing would promise a certain continuity which would save her from complete breakdown (GN456).

By narrating divergent life-events in her diary, Anna is able to provide a continuity to her life-story which otherwise would remain fragmented. Diary writing and journal-keeping are autobiographical acts that are strategically therapeutic. According to Anthony Giddens, a person's identity is to be found "in the capacity to keep a particular narrative going and ... continually integrate events which occur in the external worlds, and sort them into the ongoing 'story' about the self" (54). Porter H. Abbott also sees journal-keeping as a therapeutic practice. He says that, "with the advent of psychoanalysis, its stress is on unconscious self ... the keeping of diary has become a common therapeutic practice" (107). In his analysis, Jung's psychoanalytic concept, 'active imagination', is similar to the experience of keeping a diary, and both can be seen as similar therapeutic strategies. Pennebaker also emphasizes that diary writing is a therapeutic act which is similar to an analytic session, in which the analyst and the analysand work together to integrate divergent experiences into a coherent and meaningful narrative in order to see the analysand's life as a whole ("Telling a Story: the Health Benefits of Narrative"1248). At the same time, diary writing, although close to an analytic session in effect, is an individual act in which the writer alone works for constructing-self-narrative by interpreting past events and past selves. For example, Anna experiences her diary writing as an analytic session, which helps hercreate new interpretations of her past in the context of the present, with an expectation of the future instead of the temporal nature of her *self* (GN 459).

Anna's diary writing is a self-reflective act by which she is able to maintain a dialogic self, which certainly saves her from total self-disintegration in her schizophrenic experience. For example, in the later stage of her breakdown, which appears close to schizophrenia, Anna interacts solely through her diaries; and it definitely saves her from complete breakdown by enabling her to maintain a self-reflective and dialogical interaction within her.

Anna's search for self-healing further extends beyond intrapersonal and intra-subjective realmsand move towards the interpersonal and the inter-subjective. While the act of dreaming, diary-writing and notebook-keeping are her intrapersonal narrative strategies that work towards her self-healing, certain interpersonal relationships she establishes are therapeutic, which provide her insight into her various inner conflicts. In *The Golden Notebook* it is Anna's realization of her identity crisis and her 'writer's block' that make her come to the Jungian psychoanalyst, Mrs. Marks, for help. Anna believes that her interactions with a second person would relieve her from her inner breakdown.

Although Lessing explores the possibilities of interpersonal alliances and their role in self-healing in many of her other writings, this is the first time she brings into analysis the analyst-analysand patterning within a clinical context. The interaction between Anna and Mrs. Marks creates the analyst-analysand alliance, one of themost significantmotifsof the novel.Furthermore, their interaction acts as a pattern for other interpersonal interactions which are carried outwithin the novel. Mrs Mark advises Anna to keep a diary, and then, to note down her experiences she has both in sleep and wakefulness. Consequently, Anna begins to keep diverse events in her diary, which also include the dialogues taking place between herself and Mrs. Marks during the analytical sessions.

Anna's visit to Mrs. Marks and her psychoanalytic sessions with her could be seen as a continuation of the intrapersonal dialogues that take place within her, and her analysis of her own interpersonal relationships. This analytical interaction occurs between Anna's self-narrative attempts earlier through fiction and journal-keeping, and the therapeutic interaction which she would establish with Saul Green later. For example, shefeels that her sessions with Mrs. Marks are mere repetitions of her experiences during fiction-writing and journal-keeping: "All you've done is to bring me, step by step, to the subjective knowledge of what I knew before" (GN 227). The Anna-Saul shared experience here matches an analyst-analysand relationship established on narrative therapy, which suggests that at deeper levels, psychoanalytic interaction is an enquiry of two persons into a person's subjectivity(Aron 148).Anna's experience also goes in line with the hermeneutic perspectivethat considers psychoanalytic interaction as two- persons' shared attempt to reconstruct the self-story of an individual (Aron285).

Although Lessing is keen on examining the therapeutic possibilities of interpersonal relationships in many of her writings, it is in *The Golden Notebook*where she deals closely with the working of an 'analytical relationship'. For example, a part of Anna's diary entirely deals with her interaction with Mrs. Marks. In addition to the interaction, Anna records in her diary the interpersonal experience she establishes with Mrs. Marks. Anna-Marks relationship can be seen on the 'cause and effect'aspect of their attachment. After her interaction with Marks, Anna watches the dominant-mother's image in her dream, which she acknowledges as that of Mrs. Marks. Anna notes down in her diary that "in the dream was Mrs. Marks, very large and powerful; like a kind of amiable witch ...." (GN 239).

As has been stated before, Anna's interaction with Mrs. Marks foreshadowsthe central motif, i.e. the interaction between Anna and Saul Green. In the novel, Saul Green, the young American,appears as Anna's lover. Several similarities lie between them. For example, both of them identify themselvesas writers who at present arestruggling against the'writer's block'. Striking similaritiescan be noticed in their experiences, which are emphasized in many places in the novel. For example Saul tells Anna thatalthough they are different as individuals, much of their experience is similar (GN 540). Similarly they attribute their breakdownto their similar life experiences (GN 542).

Anna-Saul relationship reflects their interdependence. There is an element of mutuality in their relationship, which is reflected from the beginning of their relationship. Their relationship never becomes one-sided, but becomes meaningful to both. It is Saul who recognizes their interdependence first. He says: "This is me Saul Green, and I'm not happy, and never have been. So I'm making use of you. That's right. Fair exchange of making use of me" (GN 539). The phrase "making use of each other" resonates in several placesof their interaction, whichreveals much of what happens between them. Saul tells Anna: "We're both lonely people, let's be good to each other" (GN 535); "English woman! Fair! Everyone makes use of each other" (GN 548). Later Anna also recognizes their interdependence.To Anna her interaction with Saul Green acts as a mirror, which projects her own schizoid condition. In *The Golden Notebook*Anna's affair with Saul explicitly signifies the possibility of aninteraction between two schizoid individuals, which is analysed in detail by Lessing.

Anna recognizes Saul's inability to keep the order of events and the split personalities he projects. Sheconveys this to Dr. Paynter, a psychiatrist, by asking him"what was wrong with someone who had no sense of time, and seemed to be several different people" (GN 548). However, he takes Anna as the real patient, thinking that she was talking about her own problem, and suggests that she consult him.At first, Anna deniesPaynter's advice thinking that she was mistaken, and tells about this toSaul. However, soon after, she recognizes her own schizoid condition and her gradual loss of sense of time: "I realized that, like Saul, I no longer had a sense of time" (GN 567). This realization is wholly the effect of her relationship with Saul, who projectsher state of madness. She comes to the new knowledge that they are both mad, and aretrapped "in the cocoon of madness" (GN 549, 556). She not only projects the state of her madness in Saul Green, but also her own negative personality traits. In their highly symbiotic relationship, Anna Wulf and Saul Green project their never flagging cycle of aggression, cruelty, jealousy, guilt, and passion.

Their relationship brings out both the positive and negative traits of their personality.Their friendliness switches to hate in the middle of their conversation. Likewise the house, which is an oasis of their loving affection, suddenlyturns into a battle groundin such a way that the walls vibrate with hate (GN 549). There are intermittent emotional outbreaks of aggression, cruelty, jealousy, guilt, and passion in their relationship. Certainly, the readers may attribute these negative personality traits to Saul Green as 'man's cruelty inflicted upon woman', which appears as a significant theme of the novel.

However, Anna later recognizes that she is the counterpart of Saul, and in their relationship one completes the other;and that without their emotional and physical union none of them can achieve self-fulfilment. She recognizes her as "the malicious male-female dwarf figure, the principle of joy-in-destruction", and Saul as hercounterpart, "male-female, my brother and my sister ..." (GN 549). The nature of the mutuality in their relationship can be verified here, since each of them achieves self-knowledge through the other.Anna finds that just like she keeps diaries, Saul too keeps diaries, and she tries to survey his mind through them. She is now able to identify the split selves of Saul, i.e. the man she knew, and the man pictured in the diary. Moreover, she realizes that her own reading of her diaries was not revealing as her reading of Saul's dairy: "then I remembered that when I read my notebooks I didn't recognize myself. Something strange happens when one reads oneself. That is, one's self direct, not one's self projected" (GN 545). Thus Anna realizes that they need each other for self identifying their split selves of them they are blind of, and their journey into their selves can bemade by the detour via the other.

Within their dyadic relationship, both Anna and Saul recognize their roles. However, again, the roles they play are not fixed but transferable and emphasize their interdependence. For example, Saul wants Anna to act her role as an analyst who canuse her experience with Mrs. Marks. He invites Annato make use of him "to create a Hollywood dream of happiness", and in return he is going to use her "experience of witch doctors" (GN 548). Similarly, Saul tells Anna that he does not need to waste money on a psychiatrist when hecan get thetreatment from her, without any payment (GN 548).

The role Anna plays with Saul Green assumes an analytical pattern. At the same time, the analyst-analysand pattern in the Anna-Saul relationship does not solely rest on Saul's statement that he is using Anna in the role of an analyst. Anna, as invited by Saul, or willingly, acts her role as an analyst with him who plays his role as an analysand. In fact, they engage in transference relationships, as Saul transfers various roles onto Anna. For example, Anna interprets Saul's intermittent emotions of hatred and love towards her as a projection of his unconscious conflict with mother. She tells Saul:

> Like all Americans you've got mother trouble. You've fixed on me for your mother. You have to outwit me all the time, it's important that I should be outwitted. ...Then, when I get hurt, your murderous feelings for me, for the mother, frighten you, so that you have to comfort and sooth me. ... (555)

Similarly, Anna expresses the curiosity of an analyst. Just like an analyst she enters deep into Saul's madness: "I understood I'd gone right inside his craziness" (561). For example, Anna's reading of Saul's diary is her attempt to survey his mind and his unconscious conflicts.

By playing various roles with Saul Green in their relationship, Anna achieves a sense of self-fulfilment. To elaborate, Anna's act of playing roles helps her to realize her various *selves* better. For example, she realizes the self-fulfilment she achieves while playing various roles of a woman with Saul Green:

> It was like living in a hundred lives. I was astonished at how many of the female roles I have not played in life, have refused to play, or were not offered to me. Even in sleep I knew I was being condemned to play them now because I had refused them in life. (GN 576)

In fact, their relationship appears close to the transference relationship which is the very characteristic of analytic relationship: "The analyst becomes an emotional substitute for mother or father, and becomes the target of the patient's childhood fantasies, fears, desires, and defences" (Smith 110).

As mentioned above the analyst-analysand role Anna plays with Saul is reciprocal. At the latter part of their relationship, the analyst's role is shifted from Anna to Saul Green. The changing of roles is obvious when Saul recognizes Anna's 'writer's block'and coerces her to finish her novel. He tells her that unless she writes the story, she is going to crack up (GN 600). Here Saul plays the role ofthe analyst, as he recognizes Anna's need to overcome her writer's block which is necessaryfor her breakthrough. He also recognizes that Anna's triumph over her writer's block is part of his own breakthrough:

'You're going to write that book, you're going to write it, you are going to finish it'. I said: 'Why is it so important to you that I should?''Ah,' he said, in self-mocking despair. 'A good question. Well, because if you can do it, then I can'. (GN 610)

He said: 'Why do you have four notebooks?'I said: 'Obviously, because it's been necessary to split myself up, but from now on I shall be using one only'. I was interested to hear myself say this, because until then I hadn't known it (sic).(GN 571)

Their attachment develops in the relational pattern of psychoanalysis. Relational psychoanalysis emphasizes the therapeutic power of a dialectical process which is the result of a new experience rooted in a new relationship. What is expected in this new relationship is the two individuals' interdependence of each other. First, it is the mutuality or their interdependence that works as the most striking element behind their relationship. Both of them find their attachment equally meaningful.

Interpersonal alliances and their role in self-recovery can also be seen as the fundamental theme in *The Summer Before the Dark* (sic). Similar to Anna's, Kate's recovery can also be attributed to the therapeutic relationship she establishes with the young girl Maureen. The novel highlights Kate's self-quest which is represented in the two parallel journeys she makes at the same time. The first one is realistic, while the second is highly symbolic and packed with spiritual and mythical overtones. In the realistic journey, she leaves her husband and children to take up her new job as a translator,develops a passionate affair with a young man named Jeffry, and travels with him to Istanbul, where Jeffry first, and then Kate, fall mysteriously ill. While coming back desperately to London she comes into a close relationship with Maureen, a young girl of her daughter's age.

The above being her experiencein realisticjourney, on the other side, she embarks a spiritual or mythical journey which she experiences through her ongoing dream about the seal. Her perilous journey to the North Sea to revitalize the dying seal appears too desperate. However,for Kate, her short stay with Maureen turns to be a self-revealing and self-defining experience. Her desperate search for self-identity finally comes true within this relationship. The story ends with Kate's return to her family with her newly defined identity.

Structurally, Kate-Maureen relationship evolves in the same pattern as Anna-Saul relationship. First of all, like Anna-Saul relationship Kate-Maureen relationship is anchored on their interdependence. The cause and effect of their relationship is not one-sided but reciprocal, as both of them experience their relationship as equally self-revealing and self-defining. For example, Maureen is trapped in a sort of entanglement which obstructs her from defining her individual identity and will. Maureen's childhood fixation and the resulting confusion with the choice of marriage express her inability to construct her self-identity and thereby confirm her will. However, she experiences her relationship with Kate as really transforming; and by that, she is able to resolve her innerconflict.

The element of mutuality or interdependence in the Kate-Maureen relationship, like the Anna-Saul relationship, is also found in the roles they play. Maureen takes the role of an active listener and encourages Kate to narrate her life-story. Thus, their interaction creates an analytic atmosphere where Maureen acts as the co-constructor of Kate's life-story (SBD 212). Their roles as story teller and active listener evolve subtly as the critical juncture in Kate's self-recovery (SBD 213).

Maureen acts the analyst's role by encouraging Kate to revise her problematic life-story that actually leads to Kate's self-recovery. For example, it is Maureen who recognisesKate's problem andliberates her who is hopelessly stuck with Mary. Without Maureen's interference Kate is unable to retrieve her life-story from the story of Mary. This can be made emphatically clear by citing the scene in which Maureen empowers Kate to overcome the story of Mary to which she has stuck:

> When Kate told the girl about Mary, she had not realized she was putting an end to *Tell me a story, please tell a story, Kate!"…* Maureen said: "Do you realize? Your stories. We like different things. What you like is to tell about your children when they were very young. That's what you remember best. That's what you wanted to tell me, and when I wanted you to talk about being happy with Michael, you had to tell me Mary". (SBD 219-20)

5

Self-Writing and Self-Healing in Fictional Autobiography

Here our focus will be on Lessing's attempt to narrate a fictional autobiographythrough her work *The Memoirs of a Survivor*. Herremarks about her work*The Memoirs of a Survivor* as "A Dream Autobiography" and "An Attempt at an Autobiography," demandincluding this particular work in the present study (UMS 28-29). Her descriptions of her life-events in *The Memoirs* look different from the autobiographical accounts she presents in *Under My Skin*. A comparison of these alternative versions that also appear in many of her other writings would substantiate her therapeutic attempts through narrative revisions. We will also verify Lessing's repudiation of generic distinctions and her view of the universality of personal experience. This suggests that her view of autobiography is not confined within petty personal accounts,but that she is broadminded enough to consider her experiences in universal dimensions.

Lessing's style of crossing conventional genre distinctions is well evident in *The Memoirs of a Survivor*. There is considerable controversy among critics as to which genre *The Memoirs*belongs to.Realism, fantasy, fable, allegory, science fiction,and inner space fiction have been suggested

(Dooley 2). We will also consider Lessing's ambivalence in generic expressions in *The Memoirs*, and think whether 'fictional autobiography' can be a suitable term to address this work.

Lessing's intention for a cross genre experiment is evident in the four titles she has given to this work. These alternative titles confuse her readers a lot, sincethese titles may organise her work under three distinctive genres. At first she titled her work as *The Journal of a Survivor*. Then, she changed the title into *The Memoirs of aSurvivor* with the subtitle, *An Attempt on Autobiography*. She alsocalled it "anovel" (UMS28-29). These alternative titles permit herreaders and critics to suggestdifferent interpretations to the work. Awork in a particular genre may induce a significant meaning change whenrepresented in another genre. Thus, the writer's choice of theappropriate genre may predict the meaning he/she intends to createthrough the work. For example, a reader can note what differentmeanings Lessing would create when she represented her work underfour alternative titles. Zinsser says:

> Unlike autobiography, in *memoir*, a person describes a portion of his/her life. A memoir writer takes his/her readers to a narrowed part of life. This is quite different from *autobiography*, which moves in a dutiful line from birth to death, omitting nothing. *A memoirwriter* assumes much and ignores most of his/her life. Thus a memoir gives a narrowed focus with exceptional descriptions such as long passed childhood events, wars and travels. Memoir gives the writer far more fictional possibilities than autobiography(emphasis added).(11)

The title *The Memoirs of a Survivor* with the subtitle*An Attempt at Autobiography* expresses Lessing's intention of blending two genres, autobiography and memoir, with fictional dimensions. The title *memoir* seems to predict Lessing's intention of creating a fictionalized version of her autobiography.

Next, the narrative style of *The Memoirs of a Survivor* is confusing in that it is difficult to label the work as a novel, memoir,or autobiography. Certain characteristics of *The Memoirs*'narrative influence the readers to consider it as fiction. For example, it is a curious mixture of surrealism and realism. It is set in an indeterminate time and place, somewhere in the future, and in some unspecified large city. In *Under My Skin*Lessing talks of this:

> To me nothing seems more simple than the plan of this novel. A middle-aged person –the sex does not matter –observes a young self grow up. A general worsening of conditions goes on, as has happened in my life time…These are the wars and movements like Hitler, Mussolini, Communism, white supremacy, systems of brutal ideas that seem for a time unassailable, then collapse. (UMS 28-29)

Unlike a work of autobiography, *The Memoirs* does not promise any singularidentity for the author, the narrator and the protagonist.The first person narrator is anonymous throughout the work, and she maintains a distinct identity apart from the protagonist, Emily, who is mostly addressed in the third person.

The narrative, although in the first person in most places, occasionally shifts to the third person, with a fictional dimension. *The Memoirs* begins with the narrator's account of events happening around her. The narrator is put in charge of a young adolescent girl named Emily. Earlyparts of the work introducethe first person narrativethat is typical to that of a memoir or autobiography. However, in certain places of *The Memoirs*, readers can notice the narrative shiftsby which the first person narrator puts on theguise of anarrator of fiction, who effortlessly explores the protagonist's psyche by exploring the third person narrative. This narrative shiftis pointed out by Zinsser as "the narrators' attempt to separate the real world of every day waking life from her younger selves' dream world" (11).

In this work Lessing has invented an intra-homodiegetic narrator (witness narrator) who participates in the story which she narrates; even as she makes it seem that her role in her own story is subsidiary. The narrator of this memoir acts like a fiction-writer, and at the same time, she chooses the first person point of view to adhere to the conventions of the autobiographical genre. Autobiographical conventionsare also kept by omitting the narrator's proper name,both in the title and in the body of the text. The narrator deliberately obscures or masks her identity (identicalness) with that of Emily, who is constantly referred to by the narrator in the third person. Therefore the narrator's participation in her own narrative is covert. Lejeune explains this masking device or reference to the self in third person, which he calls "the soft pedal", and he saysthat it is related to the autobiographical form (32-33).

Lessing enhances the confusion again by introducing ananonymous first person narrator who records two planes of consciousness. The narrator minimizes the overtness of her participation by fabricating an identity for herself, which is distinct from Emily, the character who represents the narrator's younger self. In an interview, Lessing says about the narrative of *The Memoirs*, which is a mixture of reality and dream, marked off by the wall, complement each other and gives an all-encompassing vision about the narrator's past. She continues to say that what the narrator watches behind the wall,and "the apparent dream world actually represent her own life, her own childhood. In the tangible world, Emily whom she sees growing up represents the image of her adolescence" (Rousseau 147-8).

Critics notice a number of external evidences to support the autobiographical nature of *The Memoirs.*There are obvious resemblances between the characters in *The Memoirs*and the personalities in Lessing's autobiography, *Under My Skin*, the book which came out after two decades after the publication of *The Memoirs*. For example, the experiences of Emily, the protagonist in *The Memoirs*resembles the young Doris, who appears in*Under My Skin.* Dooley comments thatEmily's childhood beyond the wall is a vivid recreation of Lessing's own early years in Persia, and the adolescent Emily in the 'real' world of the novel is recognizable as the clever, polite uncommunicative teenager who grew up to become Doris Lessing (2).

Similarly, Emily's mother as projected in the dream flashbacks in *The Memoirs*resemblesMaude McVeagh, Lessing's mother. In addition to this, there are a number of parallel scenes in *The Memoirs*and *Under My Skin*, which are identical except for the changesin names and the differences in perspectives. Both works analyse Lessing's experiences such as her father's "tickling game" (UMS 31; MS 76); and the scene in which, the young child (Lessing), in front of her father, overhears her mother complaining about her to a friend (MS 61; UMS 30).Similarly, in bothworks,'thebaby' (Lessing's younger brother) is presented to his sister (Lessing) by their nurse, (Marta) and the young girl is told that her brother is her baby (even as she is forced to accept the lie that she is holding him, while she knows the nurse wasbearingmost of his weight) (MS 119; UMS24). Both texts also narrate the same scene in which the somewhat older, feverish daughter begsher mother to "come and cuddle me, come and cuddle me" (UMS 125-26; MS80).Furthermore, descriptions of the Tehran nursery in which Lessing was raised until her family moved to Southern Rhodesia, and then descriptions of the soldier father, the pampered baby brother, and the overworked, cold mother, are strikingly similar in the two works.

Lessing admits her autobiographical intention in writing *The Memoirs of a Survivor*. In *UnderMy Skin*Lessing calls ither "dream autobiography", and thereby she designates for the reader the autobiographical space in which the world-behind-the-wall portions can beread. Shesays that itwas her great desire for years to"write a book, a personal history ... told through dreams", and "this idea of a dream autobiography became the world behind the wall in *Memoirs of a Survivor*" (UMS 29). She also reveals her intention of creating it as a fictional project. She says how she has fictionalized it, particularly the nursery in Tehran, and the characters of her parents, both exaggerated and enlarged, because this was appropriate for the world of dreams (UMS 29).

Similarly, Lessing reiterates in interviews and on speakingtours (prior to *UnderMy Skin*and following the publication of *The Memoirs*)that *The Memoirs*was "An attempt at an Autobiography" (Rubenstein 6; Cedestrom 170). Likewise, she criticizes herpublishers who have omitted the subtitle *An Attempt at anAutobiography*, and thereby rejected the work being her autobiography (UMS 28). Here, she suggests that while writing an autobiography oneneed not to follow its conventions strictly, but rather it can be "hinted" at and "alluded"to and, "shadowed forth in a glass darkly" (UMS 29). Hence, Ellen Peel considers *The Memoirs of a Survivor* as "Lessing's astonishing classification of a book that few would even call autobiographical fiction which means that we must open ourselves to a more variegated definition of autobiography" (5).

Thus, the difficulty ofgivinga clear-cut genre distinction to *The Memoirs of a Survivor*demandsthat wequery the possibilities of considering this work as Lessing's autobiographical fiction. Choosing this approach would integrate the two divergent concepts which have already been deducted out of Lessing's writing in the previous two chapters. On the one hand, the title *autobiographical fiction* would consider the possibility of considering *The Memoirs*as Lessing's autobiographical project, which will re-emphasize the fictional nature of Lessing's autobiography, as discussed in the third chapter. On the other side, *The Memoirs of a Survivor*can also be seen from its fictional dimension, and therefore this work can beconsidered as a fictional work, telling the story of the central fictional character. *The Memoirs*, like many other fictional works of Lessing, tells the story of the protagonist and her quest for self-healing. Thus, considering *The Memoirs*as the story of its protagonist would substantiate Lessing's treatment of the theme of self-quest and self-healing in her fictional works, as mentioned in the fourth chapter.

Lessing'scomments about the autobiographicalintention of *The Memoirs* thatshe has explored her experiences in the nursery in Tehran, and by analysing the characters of her parents, still with exaggerations, she hasmadethe work appropriate to the world of her dreams (UMS 29). Thus, a new perspective towards the workcan be developed when Lessing's above statements are read with the comments she made of*The Memoirs*later:

> For years I had wondered if I could write a book, a personal history, but told through dreams, for I remember dreams well, and sometimes have kept note of them ...This idea of a dream autobiography became the world behind the wall in *Memoirs of a Survivor*" .
> (UMS 29)

Thus, by attempting*The Memoirs*asher 'dream autobiography' Lessing must have intended a fictional attempt at autobiography or a fictional autobiography.

While considering *The Memoirs of a Survivor* as Lessing's autobiographic project, the first characteristicthat strikes the reader is the similarity between the anonymous narrator in *The Memoirs*and the narrator of *Under My Skin,* who is Lessing herself. The anonymous narrator explores the narrative strategy (the analyst-analysand relationship) which Lessing herself exploreswhile narrating her autobiography in *Under My Skin.*

A close reading of *The Memoirs*would reveal that Emily, the protagonist, addressed in the third person, is the younger self of the first person anonymous narrator. For example, Loreli Cederstrom argues that, "Emily symbolizes the protagonist's (narrator's) younger personality, a repository of her youthful attitudes, an element of her development" (175). She also says that Emily is not a separate person,but only designates the childhood self of the narrator (176). Throughout *The Memoirs*Emily projects her various selves, both in the real and in the dream world.Such a narrative strategy positions the narrator in a witness position, and Emily, who is the narrator's younger self, in a third person position. However, apart from her identity as a witness, the narrator is merged with the subjectivity of Emily.The narrator addresses her identity as *I*, the narrating self, in the beginning of the story.Shortly after the arrival of Emily, she begins to be subjected beyond the wall to a child's eye-view of an oppressed nursery, where personal scenes of the childhood of Emily and her brother are played out. The narrator of *The Memoirs*describes this experience:

> Being invited into this scene was to be absorbed into child-space; I saw it as a small child might – that is enormous and implacable; but at the same time I kept with me my knowledge that it was tiny and implacable – because petty, unimportant".(MS 40)

The dream sequences in *The Memoirs* reveal Emily's past. The breaking down of the real world with the occasional emergence of the dream world reveals that Emily is the younger self of the narrator. When the narrator enters the world of dreams, she recognizes that Emily's past is her own "personal" realm (MS 38).

The narrator who watches Emily in the dream world sees herself. To the narrator, the dissolving dream wall takes her to a self-revelatory experience. She calls her dreams of Emily her "personal experiences" that assault her conscious memories (MS 38). The narrator experiences the dream scenery as she had actually experienced them in real life.Similarly, the narrator experiences a sense of nostalgia while watching Emily's house in her dream (MS 38). The dreamsin which she watches Emily are very personal to her, as they reveal her own past, her past selves. She realizes thather own past, which is revealed through these dreams, is a "prison" with "unalterable law of time"(MS 39).Lessing comments of the narrator's experience in an interview:

> In *Memoirs of a Survivor*, what the narrator believes that she is watching behind the wall, that apparent dream world, actually represents her own life, her own childhood. In the tangible world, Emily whom she sees growing up represents the image of her adolescence. Thus reality and dream, marked off by the wall, complement each other to give an all encompassing vision to the narrators' past.(Rousseau147-48)

In *The Memoirs*, these dream sequences enable the narrator to fix her distinct past selves in Emily.

However, in the 'realistic' part of the story, the narrator fabricates an identity for herself, which is distinct from Emily, the character who represents the narrator's younger self. The narrating voice attempts to separateher identity from the narrated subject whom she calls 'Emily' by addressing herself as 'I'. Moreover, in *The Memoirs,* Emily is projectedinher different selves, both in the real world and in the dream world. In the real world, Emily appears as a distinct character, who is put under the care of the middle-aged narrator by a middle-aged man whose relationship with the child is not mentioned. He says: "She is Emily Cartright. Look after her" (MS 17). The narrator tells of her that "she was a large child, of about twelve. Not a child, really; but in that half-way place where soon she would be a girl" (MS 22). From the child's self, by the end of the story she grows upunnaturally to a woman who projects the image of a mother (MS 108). The narrator addresses her by different names whichprojectsher various selves: "The bright attractive girl" (MS 63); "you a big girl" (MS 81). She watches Emily's various selves: "She came back with some second hand clothes that in one giant's step took her from being a child with fantastic versions of herself in to a girl – a woman rather"(MS 54). Similarly, the narrator observes her growing body, her physical attractiveness and her developing sexuality (MS 22, 27). Next, Emily projects her different selves in her relationships with others, particularly with her lover Gerald, her friend June, and her pet Hugo. Her relationship with Gerald places her in the more matured self of a parent. Emily and Gerald are seen as parents (MS 147). She takes the self of an emotional mother with June (MS 108). Her closeness with her pet, Hugo, affixes onher a child's self.

Similarly, in the dream world, the narrator watches Emily in her various childhood selves. She sees Emily as: "a small girl about four "(MS 31);" the little girl"(MS 40); " the child "(MS 41);" the small child" (MS 42); "mixture of the child and the young girl" (42). Thus both in the real world and in the dream world Emily projects her different selves, which the narrator watchesat close quarters.

Lessing's way of separating the central character's distinct selves in *TheMemoirs of a Survivor* is very much similar to Lessing's first volume of autobiography *Under My Skin,* where she fixes her younger selves by distinct names, and watches them as distinct personalities ever present within her. She also makes narrative shifts while addressing her childhood selves. For example, in *Under My Skin,* she shifts her first person narrative voice into the third person as though she is working with fiction. For example, she recreates her early childhood selves in *Under My Skin*: "First the tiny girl and then the baby…Harry is a good little baba, Doris is a good little baba…Doddis is a good baba" (UMS 27). Similarly, Lessing reconstructs her childhood selves whileimaginatively narrating her train journey with her parents: "A small girl sits on the train seat with her teddy" (UMS 43). Here, by the third personal address, "A small girl with her teddy" Lessing is fixing one of her childhood selves. Similarly, Lessing addresses herself in disguise: "The little girl" (UMS 80). Next, in the same work, Lessing presents her adolescent self, Tigger Tayler (UMS 106, 107,109, 112,199). She acknowledges them as multiple selves in her personality (UMS 261).

In *The Memoirs,* the narrator attempts to fix her childhood selves in Emily, and thatlooks similar to Lessing's own attempt to detach her past selves in *Under My Skin,*which in turn would substantiateher attempt at self-analysis by exploring the analyst-analysand patterning inwritings. She acknowledges the exclusive therapeutic purpose of the above narrative technique (UMS 12).

Thus, Lessing's narrative strategy that she talks of above and experiments with both in *Under My Skin* and in *The Memoirs of a Survivor*confirm the possibility of manipulating the analyst-analysand strategy in self-representational writing. In *Under My Skin,* this technique is simple, and can be considered asmere playfulness or idiosyncrasy of the author, as Lessing herself is the narrator there, who merely addresses her childhood selves by different names. On the other hand, in *The Memoirs*the anonymous narrator is more or less a distinct character who fixes her childhood selves in a distinct character, Emily. Thus, this kind of narrative technique emphasizes Lessing's exploration of an analyst-analysand patterning in her writings in general.

Lessing considers writing more as a personal affair. She explores various therapeutic possibilities in writing. *The Memoirs of a Survivor* can be regarded as a better example for this. Through this fictional autobiography she experiments with a fictional enquiry into her life. Her unconventionalities and idiosyncrasiesare quite evident in *The Memoirs,* as her treatment of her own life is in this work is so differentfrom *Under My Skin* and her other self-representational writings. Autobiographic elements are bizarrely presented, and as a result, the work creates numerous ambiguities. The world of *The Memoirs* appears far morestrange to the reader who has watched the world in *Under My Skin.* One possible reason for this incongruity is that it is a protection which Lessing has taken during her autobiographical narration. She speaks of this in *Under My Skin*:

> ... You will never get access here,you can't, this is the ultimate and inviolable privacy.They call it loneliness, that here is this place unsharable with anyone at all, ever, but it is all we have to fall back on... (UMS 20)

The narrative of *The Memoirs* is broken into two spheres, the real world and the dream world.

A realistic story is narrated in the real world, which at the beginning looks simple, but gets complicated with the introduction of surreal flash backs. Interestingly, the events narrated in the surreal flashbackscenes are Lessing's own autobiographical accounts. Thiscomplicates the text,as the events presented in the story arethe experiences of Emily, the fictional character, as well as that of the witness, the anonymous narrator. Furthermore, the confusion is intensified due to the complexity in verifying Lessing's autobiographical elements, as they are narrated in astrange dream language.

However, the striking feature that suggests*The Memoirs*as Lessing's autobiography is the obvious attempt she has made to revise some of herlife events in this work. Her self-representational writings give her far more scope for self-analysis and self-healing than that an autobiographer can achieve from his/her writing. She achieves thisby continuously revising her life-story. Critics and many of her readers allege that most of her writings are mere repetitions (Hazeleton; Dooley 3). They complain that similar themes are repeatedly treated in almost all her works. However, by close observation it can be noted that she actually intends it. For example, she states her intentionof autobiographicrevision, which may be attributed as the reason for the intentional repetition:

> Telling the truth or not telling it, and how much, is a lesser problem than the one of shifting perspectives, for you see your life differently at different stages, like climbing a mountain while the landscape changes with every turn in the path... (UMS 12)

Her willingness to change perspective from time to time points out her intention of autobiographic revision, which is afundamental goal of narrative therapy. The above statement made by Lessing also confirms that she is continuing her search of autobiographical truth, and the autobiographical nature of her writing cannot be limitedto the two volumes of her autobiography.

This can be verified with a comparative analysis of theautobiographical events presented both in *Under My Skin* and *The Memoirs of a Survivor*. For example, in *Under My Skin* Lessing attempts to revise many of her life eventsthat she narrates in *The Memoirs*. It is interesting to find how sheconstructs two dissimilar versions of her life events in these works, which were written in the gap of four decades.

This narrative revision provides Lessing self-healing, which a conventional autobiographer may not achieve through his/her writings. Through continuous revisions of her life-story, she creates alternative versions of the reality of her past. Moreover, by revising her self-story, which is itself re-interpretation, she is able to construct a 'healedself'. Narrative revisions also help her to construct and reconstruct a morally sound, meaningful, and healthy self within her. Besides, by the act of revising she fills the gaps of her self-story, and makes it more coherent by developing a beginning, middle, and end. Herstrategy here is very close to the concepts of narrative psychology; they emphasise that anindividual can healher *self* by the act of re-telling and reconstructing it in a morally healthy way. For example, the pattern of 'self-healing by self-change' as introduced by Freeman goes parallel to that ofLessing's strategy. Freemansuggests that, through the act of self-narration, theindividual can interpret her traumatic life events from different perspectives, and thereby create various versions of them.These are the alternativeversionsfrom which the individual can choose a healthier and morally superior one (3-18). It is this narrative act that works as therapeutic, and leads to self-healing.

In *The Memoirs* Lessingachieves self-healing bycreating various versions of traumatic life-events, and choosing the healthiest among them.The surreal flashback scenes in *The Memoirs*reveal the early conflicted relationships between the child Emily and her dominant mother. The nursery scene in *The Memoirs*is similar to Lessing's descriptions of her experiences in the Tehran nursery in *Under My Skin*. This reveals that sheattempts to analysethe conflicted relationship with her mother in *The Memoirs* closely.

However, there are dissimilarities in perspectives and emotions while narrating the same events in the two works. For example, in *The Memoirs*the narrator watches Emily's mother:

> Dominant among them was a woman, one I had seen before, knew well. She was tall, large, with clean-china healthiness, all blue eyes, pink cheeks, and the jolly nonsense mouth of school girl. ... (MS 60)

In *Under My Skin* Lessing narrates a different version of the above scene: "My mother was enormous, solid, a vibrating column of efficiency and ruthless energy, and part of my attention was always on her, for I was afraid she would carelessly knock me over, tread on me" (UMS 27-28). To compare the emotions expressedin the two accounts, the first one is seen as a dream account, which reveals the child's unconscious fears and aversions projected on the domineering and powerful mother. This projects the mind's unconscious elements, revealing the hidden conflictsbetween the child and her mother. The unpolished language of the dream reveals the child's unconscious fear of, and aversion to, the authoritarian mother figure. However, in the scene in *Under My Skin*, unlike the first, the language is more polished, which fits the description of the conventional manners and mores that determine the mother-daughter relationship.

Again, in the Nursery scene, as revealed in dream flashbacks in *The Memoirs*, readerscan watch how Lessing subtly narrates a version of another hurting memory from early childhood:

> The baby was laughing. The mother wanted to take the baby from the nurse, but the nurse held tight and said: 'Oh no, this one, this is my baby, he's my baby'. 'Oh no, Nurse,' said the strong tower of a mother, taller than anything in the room, taller than the big nurse, almost as high as the ceiling: 'Oh no', she said, smiling but with her lips tight, 'he's my baby'. 'No, this is my baby', said the nurse now rocking and crooning the infant, 'he's my darling baby, but the other one she's your baby, Emily is yours, madam'. (MS 40)

However, it is interesting to note that when Lessing narrates the same event in *Under My Skin*, she softensher emotional outburstagainst her mother, which she freely expresses in the above passage in *The Memoirs*. For example, instead of themorally unhealthy version in *The Memoirs*she tries to construct a morally healthier alternative in *Under My Skin*:

> I would like to know more about Marta, forced to be nursemaid in the English family. 'Old Marta'. But she doesn't look so old in the photographs. What war, calamity, famine, personal misfortune forced her to work in the strict English nursery where her sufferings and loneliness goaded her tongue and made hands hard and unkind? At least with me. 'Bebe is my child, madame. Doris is not my child. Doris is your child.But Bebe is mine'. So she said often (sic) .(UMS 27-28)

Thus, in *Under My Skin*, unlike in *The Memoirs*, Lessing moves towards a therapeutic reconciliation with her mother and Marta, the nurse, by finding an alternative and healthy reason for the nurse's behaviour. Here Lessing believes that "her sufferings and loneliness goaded her tongue and made hands hard and unkind" (UMS 28).Similarly,when Lessing reports her mother's hard words in *Under My Skin*,she changes her tone of hatred towards her mother by simply seeing her mother'sbehaviour as her "natural theatricality" (UMS 29). Lessing adds: "She might have been an actress, but I am sure that did not occur to her" (UMS 29).

Anotherautobiographical event that Lessing narrates both in *Under My Skin* and *The Memoirs of Survivor* is the 'tickling game'. However, while she narrates the same incident in the two works, she creates two alternative versions that differ from each other. For example in *Under My Skin,* she writes of this:

> Every night took place a ritual. We, the small children, were led down by the nurse for the bedtime game. We had pillow fights, were chased, caught, thrown up in the air– and tickled ... I hear the excited cries from myself and my brother and my mother as the air filled with feathers …And the moment when Daddy captures his little daughter and her face is forced down into his lap or crotch, into the unwashed smell– he never did go for washing much, and – don't forget…they smelled horrible. (UMS 31)

Lessing narrates a dream version of the same memory in *The Memoirs*:

> In a large chair set against the curtains the soldier-like man sat with his knee apart, gripping between them the small girl who stood shrieking. On his face, under the moustache, was a small tight smile. He was 'tickling' the child. This was a 'game', the bedtime 'game', a ritual. The elder child was being played with, was being made tired…now she was hot and sweating, and her body was contorting and twisting to escape the man's great hands that squeezed and dug into her ribs, to escape the great cruel face that bent so close over her with its look of private satisfaction ...(MS 76-77)

Again, a comparison of the two versions of the same event may highlight Lessing's attempt to tone down a psychologically disturbing memory. The dream version in *The Memoirs* narrates the physical and psychological sufferings of the small girl in her father's hands. Part of her emotional hurt is due to her uncaring mother who not only ignores the daughter's emotional suffering but also enjoys it witha sadistic pleasure. However, Lessing tones down the emotional intensity when she narrates the event in *Under My Skin.* She cuts down a few disturbing details for creatinga more healthy version of the event. Moreover, a noticeable narrative shift is made in the second version: "And the moment when Daddy captures his little daughter and her face is forced down ..." (31). The introduction of the words 'daddy' and 'daughter' seems as her attempt to shift the narrative position and keepher readers from identifying it asherautobiographical account. Besides that, in *Under My Skin*, unlike in *The Memoirs*, the recollection of her memory of the event is not as emotionally hurting as another. In *Under My Skin*, instead of the physical and psychological hurt, the odour of tobacco and the "unwashed" clothes are projected as carrying the unpleasantness of the event.

Narrative revision is a strategy in psychotherapy. For example, Roy Schafer, an authority in narrative psychology, emphasises the significance of revision inself-narration. He says that during self-narration the analyst and the analysand have to expect narrative revisions that can supply more meanings, sometimes contradictory meanings, and thereby more understanding to the analysand's life-story that werenot initially expected ("Listening in Psychoanalysis"). Similarly he describes howanindividual, without the help of the analyst, can resort to narrative revisions that enable to construct a therapeutic version of herlife events ("Listening in Psychoanalysis").

Likewise, Lessing achievesa therapeutic experience by constructing alternative versions of a traumatic life event in her writing. While comparing the two versionsshe has constructed (the first in *The Memoirs*, and second in *Under My Skin*) the first can be assessed as morally unhealthy, less coherentand emotionally disturbing, while second is morally healthier, more coherent and less emotionally disturbing. Moreover, unlike in *Under My Skin*, in *The Memoirs*Lessing is able to wield the mask of fiction tokeeper personal secrets from public exposure (UMS 29).

Lessing makes a more direct approach to self disclosure, in the early part of *The Memoirs*. She does the same in many of her fictional works when she remarks about her parents, particularly her mother.Lessing analyses the same experience and the hatred she had felt towards her mother because of her hard words:

> She talks all the time about what a burden her children are to her, how they take it out of her, how much she is unfulfilled and unappreciated, how no one but a mother knows how much she has to give of herself to ungrateful children who soak up her precious talents and juices like so many avid sponges. (UMS29)

In *Under My Skin* Lessing reveals how much self-hurt she had suffered within.She says thatshe was filled with the cold flame of hatred, and she could have killed her there and then (UMS 30).However, whenshenarratesthe same experience in *The Memoirs*she justifies her side clearly,by asserting herselfas blameless, as someone who was unjustly accusedby her critical mother who wanted to projecther own problemson her children.

The title 'autobiographical fiction' necessitates further verification of *The Memoirs* as a fictional work. Contrary to its implicit autobiographical nature, *The Memoirs*shares close similarities withLessing's fictional works. The work allowsthe readersto considerit as fiction, as it treats the self-evolution ofthe protagonist, Emily, as a significant narrative. The 'realistic'partof *The Memoirs* presents the self evolution of Emily. From the child's self thatEmilyowns at the beginning of the story, she achieves a woman's self at the end. The three years she spends with the narrator creates a new self within her. She achieves a new self, which is quite distinct from the one she projects at the beginning of the story.

At the beginning, Emily is introducedas a young girl who is putunder the care of the narrator by an unknown middle-aged person (MS16-17). It is quite interesting to note how Emily goes through various stages of physical, sexual, and emotional development, evolving a new self within her. Evidently, it is Emily's new relationship with the narrator that precipitates her individuation. For example, the narrator finds how Emily makes use of her for her *self*-development: "she was making use of me to check her impulse to step forward, away from childhood into being a girl, a young girl with clothes and mannerisms and words regulated precisely to that condition" (MS 43).

Like many other fictional works of Lessing, *The Memoirs* analyzes closely the diverse meanings of interpersonal relationships, and how interpersonal attachments are quite integral to self-healing. Like Lessing's other protagonists, Emily too experiences the self-healing influence of interpersonal relationships. Similarly, Lessing's treatment of interpersonal attachments in *The Memoirs* emphasizes her belief that the foundation of a person's interpersonal relationships lies in his/her early attachment with mother (Ainsworth 113). For example, in the intermittent dream flashbacks of the story Lessing illustrates howEmily's self is affected by self-disruptive elements from herattachment with her mother.At the time, in the realistic part of the story Lessingdemonstrates how Emily compensates for her interrupted emotional development, and achieves self-healing through meaningful interpersonal relationships thatwork as'alternatives'to her disrupted relationships. The new relationships are called'alternatives' since they compensate for her disrupted relationships with her mother.

Among the relationships analysed in *The Memoirs*, the narrator's relationship with Emily creates an alternative mother-daughter pattern. In her attachment with Emily,a child girl, the middle-aged narrator recognises within her a motherly self. The narrator acts as a mother to Emily. For example, she feels as though she has ceased to exist, in her own right, but considers her existenceonly as a continuation for Emily, "as her parents, or a parent, a guardian, foster parents" (MS 27). The narrator's emotion towards Emily reflects the mother's emotional attachment to her child. It gets so strong so that she is unable to separate herself from the child. For example, the narrator watches over Emily who sleeps long hours continuously, like an infant. She feels unable to leave the room:

> In those first few days she slept and slept... I was unconsciously thinking of her as younger than she was. I sat waiting quietly in my living-room, knowing that she was asleep, exactly as one does with a small child... All kinds of emotions I had not felt for a long time came to life in me again. (MS 24)

Similarly, the narrator reveals her concern for Emily,which equals that of a mother, whose heart aches for her child (MS 27).She was absorbed with Emily for her concern for her (MS 43).While watching Emily she noticesthe spurtin herphysical development, and how her adolescent sexuality brings out a new self within her. The narrator also becomes worried about Emily's relationship with the gang and her affair with Gerald, the gang leader. She alsogets deeply worried about Emily whoslowly gets detached from her: "She had no idea of course of the terror I felt for her account, the anxiety, the need to protect. She did not know that the care of her had filled my life, water soaking a sponge...but did I have the right to complain" (MS 49).The middle-aged narrator experiences her relationship with Emily astherapeuticallyself-revelatory. Her experience, like that ofLessing's other middle-aged protagonists, is self-fulfilling.

The narrator-Emily relationship can also be seen in line with the mutualityreflected in interpersonal relationships. Each of them experiences theirrelationshipas a detour via the other. The narrator meets her own past selves in Emily. Beyond the dream wall the narrator watches her own 'personal' world as opened in her dreams about Emily's childhood. Unlike in the realistic part of the story, particularly when the narrator watches beyond the dream walls, she fails toseparate her identity from Emily's. Instead, the narrator, Emily and Juneare merged into one self and their experience becomes one in essence (MS 123). For example, beyond the dream walls the narrator watches herself with Emily, and the other girl June, who eat together in the 'sugar house' (MS 123). Similarly, as the narrator watches the 'child Emily', she feels that she is getting 'absorbed' into Emily (MS43). Thus, in one part, the narrator projects herself as mother to Emily and on the other, sheprobes into her own childhood selvesthrough Emily.

As the element of mutuality is emphatically underlined in their relationship, the narrator-Emily relationship can be considered as another striking transference relationship developed between many of Lessing's characters. In the transference relationship established in therapy the analysand projects on the analyst his/her early relationship with parents.The transference relationship enables the analyst to interpret the analysand's unconscious conflicts, which are often causedby his/her troubled relationship with parents.Likewise, in *The Memoirs*, Emily's conflicts with her real mother are transferred to the narrator, whose attachment with Emily createsin the narrator a motherly self. The narrator-Emily relationship also demonstrates the conflicted relationship between the middle-aged mother and her daughter. In addition to that, through their dyadic relationship the narrator enters into her own personal world, which was hither to unknown to her, where she watches her own childhood selves. Consequently, she is not able to separate her identity and experiences from Emily's; instead she realizes them as one in essence.

As mentioned in the beginning of this chapter, many critics consider*The Memoirs* as a fable (Glendinning 1405). The surreal flashbacks scenes, the strange human-like behaviour of Hugo, Emily's petdog and his attachment toher, impartsto *The Memoirs* a fable like character. The narrator describes the strange appearance of Hugo. She says that Hugo is a dog.Sometimes she cannot say whether it is a dog or a cat, but decides it asan animal at any rate. "It was the size of a bull dog, and shaped more like a dog than a cat" (MS 22). In the story Hugo is a humanized animal. He expresses human emotions that are strange in an animal. The narrator marvels at Hugo's emotions – his fidelity, humility, and endurance – and is amazed to findthat itis not a real dog, but half humanized. But his strong blazing green eyesare foreign to man (MS 56).

The story projects Hugo's intimate attachment to Emily. This attachment is more intensely meaningful than an animal's attachment to a human being. Emily's attachment to Hugo displays the complex pattern of interpersonal attachments. Again, just like the narrator-Emily relationship it is the element of mutuality that binds the Emily-Hugo relationship. Emilysat down on the floor and "put her arms around her Hugo, and hugged him close, swaying a little… Oh no, no, no, dear Hugo,

I wouldn't, I couldn't, I wouldn't let them, don't be so frightened ...He had his head on her shoulder, in their usual way of mutual comfort at such times" (MS35).

The bond that fastenstheir relationshipis theemotional bond between a mother and her child (MS 71). Their attachment also reflects a pattern: Emily would lie all day on the sofa with her yellow dog (like a cat or cat-like dog), and she would spend all day hugging, petting, and stroking him. She would suck sweets, eat bread and jam, fondle the animal and day dream (MS 44). Emily and Hugo share many human emotions:

> She would run after them a little way with some of the other girls, and then come home, subdued, to her arms around her Hugo, her dark head down on his yellow coat. It was as if they both wept. They huddled together, creatures in sorrow, comforting each other".(MS73)

Emily acts as Hugo's protector, and he gets deeply distressed when she leaves her. The narrator describes Hugo's deep anguish when Emily left him:

> The animal sat, not beside her, but quietly in a corner. You could believe he was weeping, or would if he knew how. He sorrowed inwardly. His lids lowered themselves as crises of pain gripped him, and he would give a great shiver. When Emily went to bed she had to call him several times and he went at last, slowly...But he was in inner isolation from her. He was protecting himself. (MS 65)

Another striking attachment that is deeply analyzed in *The Memoirs* is Emily's relationship with June. In the 'realistic' part of the story, June is presented as a distinct character who acts as Emily's friend and a member in the gang. Although only two years younger than Emily, June be haves like a child. The narrator sees "two girls in a young girls' friend ship, despite one being already a woman, and one still a child, with a child's face and body" (MS 89).

Emily's self-evolution is partly indebted to her attachment to June. The bond of interdependence is still clear between Emily and June. The narrator wonderswhy"it would not be possible for Emily to be separated from June" (MS 141). She also sayshow the two girls slept in each other's arms for comfort (MS 133).The Emily-June relationship displays the roles these individuals play, as well as their interdependence. For example Emily plays the role of a mother to June (MS 94,108) as well as that of a friend (108). Similarly, Emily, who possesses an emotional authority over June,plays a dominant role: "I had never understood how much Emily depended on that thin sharp faced waif, who not only looked three years younger, but was in a different realm altogether, as different as childhood is from womanhood" (MS 122).

On the other hand, June who appears in the dream flashback scenes does not own a separate identity as a person; instead, she appears more or less one of the selves of Emily. Through a close analysis of the dream flash backs, particularly, that display Emily and June together, we can come to understand the two distinct personalities, who may also display two distinct selves of the narrator:

> There was Emily, breaking off whole pieces of the roof and cramming them into her healthy mouth; there, too, was June, languidly picking and choosing... We ate and ate our way into the house like termites, our stomachs laden but unsatisfied, unable to stop ourselves, but nauseated. (MS 123)

Lessing's autobiographicalstrategy in *The Memoirs* can be regarded as an act of *fictionalisis* (Marlatt15). In her work "Self-Representation and Fictionalisis", Marlattdiscusses the fictional part of one's autobiography as a therapeutic strategy. She says that autobiography is much similar to poetry on the ground that both are an attempt at*fictionalisis,* which is: "a self analysis that plays fictively with the primary images of one's life, a fiction that uncovers analytically that territory when fact and fiction coincide" (15). Inthe *Memoirs* Lessing seems to have engaged with such a project.

By applying the concept of fictionalisis in *The Memoirs*, the story of Emily can be considered as the imaginary part of Lessing's autobiography, bywhich she takes up the theme of mother-daughter conflict in order to analyze and resolve it. In this way, *The Memoirs* can be considered as herautobiographic enquiry into a work, which is constructed apparently as a fiction. In this work she has inextricably amalgamated her autobiography into the story of the fictional character Emily. The story of Emily and her mother enables Lessing to explore and analyze various realms of mother-daughter, mother-child relationships.Marlattadds that that the imaginary part of one's autobiography can be a therapeutic strategy (16). Schafersays that whilewriting one's *self,*the meaning is actualized through narration, by narrating stories about the *self,* relationships, the state of one's local world in the past, present and predicted future, the wide world and the imaginary worlds, and so on ("Listening in Psychoanalysis").Through the story of Emily and her mother, Lessing has constructedthe imaginary part of her own relationship with her mother.

In *Under My Skin* she tries to analyze her conflicted relationship with her mother, but instead of analyzing herintensive emotional turmoil with her mother fully, she attemptsat reconciliation. It can be assumed that Lessing preferred not to present emotionally intensive scenes (full of anger and hatred) in her autobiography, where she intended the treatment of these violent emotions to be moresubtle. For example, in *The Memoirs* she analyzes deeply the emotional turmoil that was created due to her mother's favouritism towards her brother.*In Under My Skin* the analysis is more subtle, and not so intensive as the description in *The Memoirs*. For example, she limits her emotional hurt at her mother's unforgivable favour to her brother, and the resultant hatred toa general statement. She says that her mother had not wanted a girl, but a boy, and that she knew from the beginning that her mother loved her little brother unconditionally, and that she did not love her (UMS 25). Lessing leaves that serious subject soon by saying that "by this event and others of the same kind my emotional life was forever determined" (UMS 25).

On the other hand, in *TheMemoirs*sheanalyses deeply the mother-child emotional bond (her own relationship with her mother) and explores how early breakdowns of that relationship could affect the child's (Lessing's) emotional development.*TheMemoirs* presents the recurring dream images of a mother who favours her baby boy and neglects her daughter. The boy is always her favourite, and she spends all her time drooling over him. On the other hand, she always neglects her small daughter, who craves for love and caresses from her mother. The dream images in *The Memoirs* are impregnated with many archetypal symbols that reveal the subtle realms of mother-child relationship:

> She was talking to a woman.... her eyes were blank, did not see the woman she was talking to, nor the small child in her lap, whom she bumped up and down energetically, using her heal as a spring. Nor did she see the little girl who stood a short way from the mother, watching, listening, all her senses stretched, as if every pore took in information in the form of warnings threats, messages of dislike. From this child emanated strong waves of painful emotion. It was guilt. She was condemned. And, as I recognized this emotion and the group of people there in the heavy comfortable room, the scene formalized itself like a Victorian problem picture or a photograph from an old fashioned play. Over it was written in emphatic script: GUILT. (MS 60)

The above dream scene reoccurs in different places in *TheMemoirs*:

> The child on her knee, two or three years old, a heavy passive child dressed in white wool that smelled damp, was being jogged faster now; his eyes were gazing as the world bounced up and down around him, his adenoidal mouth was open and slack, the full cheeks quivering. (61)

The dream passage above has a number of archetypal images which disclose the child's fear of her domineering mother and the deep emotional suffering she felt within her mind. She feels *guilty* as she has been rejected from her mother's love, and it is externalized in the reactions of the child. For example, the child's unconscious guilt is externalized in the images: the little girl about five or six"had her thumb in her mouth"; herface "was shadowed and bleak because of the pressure of criticism on her, her existence" (60).

By relating her own autobiography with the apparent fictional story of Emily Lessing has imparted a sense of universality to her personal experience. This emphasizes one of her stable beliefs – the universality of personal experience. She uses it to justify writing about petty personal problems "because nothing is personal, in the sense that it is uniquely one's own. Growing up is after all only the understanding that one's unique and incredible experience is what everyone shares"(GN 18). Emily, June, the narrator, and Emily's mother are all merged into one continuous being. And the character Emily, at times at least, is every woman, a victim of "the emotional hurts which are common, are the human condition, part of every one's infancy" (UMS 25).The story of *The Memoirs,* with its universal therapeutic implications, can be taken as the story of Doris Lessing and everyone else, as well as that of Emily.

Thus, through *The Memoirs of a Survivor,*Lessing has constructed*A Dream Autobiography,* as she subtitled it. Lessing's interest in exploring and analyzing her dreams and thereby realizing her unconscious conflicts are very evident in *The Memoirs.*She proves herself to be a brilliant experimenter with dreams,who knows that many of her childhood events are traumatic, which can be fixed and analyzed only by exploring her dreams.

6

Conclusion

Lessing's writing is highly marked for its unconventionalities. Her writing poses several contradictions within, and therefore she has been mostly misunderstood. She finds great interest in treating aspects that conventionally contradict each other, and those that are unconventional and less experimented with. One of these aspects is her obsessive autobiographical interest in exploring her parents' lives in almost all the works. This autobiographical quest is so persisting that as she moves from one work to another she comes back to it more forcefully than before. Her recently published *Alfred and Emily* convinces us of this fact. Although it looks and feels like a novel, this work reveals Lessing's persistent desire to explore her parents' traumatic and hopeless lives, which is also an attempt at self-exploration. This is clear in her previous autobiographical works that include the two volumes of autobiographies and a number of other semi-autobiographical works.

Lessing finds great interest in bringing together aspects that are conventionally separated. Conventional distinctions in writing become blurred in Lessing. We have seen in her works themes arranged complexly together that are conventionally polarized. For example, we notice in her the confluence of aspects such as change versus stasis, personal versus universal, individual versus collective, fact versus fiction, imaginary versus reality etc, to cite a few. She maintains that autobiography cannot guarantee (the reader) the scientific objectivity and strict referentiality that are considered the distinctive qualities of autobiography. For example, in *Under My Skin* Lessing emphatically states her intention of finding the truth. However, it has been verified that the truth she searches for is a therapeutic one, which may be more fictional than factual. Thus Lessing rejects the conventional views of autobiography.

Lessing can be called a writer with firm motives. A close observation of her works affirms that she has firm intentions behind writing, and among them, the most insistent is the therapeutic. An attempt to appraise her writing solely within the aesthetic framework would surely fail. She is one of those writers whose scope goes beyond the concepts of *art per se*. Similarly, she would only be misunderstood if we try to connect her solely to any political or ideological movement of her time. It is true that movements of her time have had their influence upon her. However, it is more convincing to view her writing within the therapeutic framework that she constructs within each of her works.

The present study has posited various reasons why Lessing attaches unconventional meanings to certain aspects; for example, her peculiar devotion to fiction and imagination, her ambiguous approach to memory, her confusing questions on the nature of the truth and reality, and her recourse to unnatural modes of perception. It has tried to resolve the above by identifying them as her therapeutic strategies.

She has a similar approach to memory. She rejects the childhood memories induced by her parents based on the view that they are unhealthy, traumatic and less cohesive, and will not help her in the construction of a healthy self. Therefore, she replaces them with imaginatively created memories that are morally healthier, more coherent and therapeutic.

Another controversial issue is the nature of Lessing's autobiography. Her treatment of autobiography is so ambiguous that it is difficult to ascertain whether it is purely confessional, or personal. Confessionality, which is the traditional attribute of autobiography, is not applicable in her case. She reveals her anti-confessional attitude both in her views and in the way she has treated her autobiographies. She considers self-writing as one's personal affair by advocating the writer's freedom and authority in manipulating fiction within the writing. However, her concept of the priority of 'personal intention' becomes more ambiguous in praxis. For example, in contrast to her concept of personal intention, (which can be associated with therapeutic intention in writing) she empha-sises elsewhere the triviality of personal of intention in writing, by emphasising the significance of universalism.

The confessional against the personal and the personal against the universal are issues in Less-ing's autobiography that can also be resolved by highlighting the therapeutic nature of her writing. She considers the therapeutic intention as more forceful than any other in her writing, whether it is confessional or personal or universal in nature. Thus, Lessing's writing has both personal and universal dimensions in the sense that it is her attempt to analyze her personal *self* along with of-fering a creative solution to her reading community to heal their selves. In that way, the personal *self* as projected and analyzed, explored and healed, not only represents Lessing's private *self*, but also a universal *self*.

Lessing's personal *selves* have also been projected in her fictional writings. Many of her protago-nists are the fictional representations of her own various *selves*. In addition to presenting many au-tobiographical events and personages in fiction, Lessing maintains a corresponding treatment both in fiction and autobiography. The most striking is her focus on the themes of self-quest and self-healing. Both her autobiography and fiction strikingly present the protagonists' identity crises and emotional breakdowns, the intuitive insights they achieve of their inner conflicts and their causes, and their individual attempts to heal their selves. This pattern of self-recovery can be seen all her works.

There are also close similarities between the therapeutic strategies adopted by Lessing and her protagonists. As she strategizes her autobiography to be therapeutic, so she strategizes her fiction to be therapeutic to the protagonists concerned. The central motif as found in Lessing's writing, both in fiction and in autobiography is the 'freedom of subjectivity', which can also be marked as one of her therapeutic strategies. In her novels she finds great interest in probing into the minds of her protagonists. However, she does not attempt an objective analysis of their minds. Instead, the analysis is so deep that it projects their subjective experiences.

Thus, the 'freedom of subjectivity', as enjoyed by Lessing's characters and projected in her writ-ing, is a marked characteristic of her novels, elucidating the acts of self-narration and self-analysis – therapeutic strategies introduced by Lessing in her works. Her protagonists are offered greater freedom to enter into their subjective realms, as Lessing herself experiences in her autobiographies. Her fictional works provide several descriptions of the protagonists' subjective experiences, such as dreams, fantasies, diary writing and introspective dialogues. However, their self-reflective experiences are not only induced by spontaneous acts like dreaming and 'fantasying', but they also achieve them by rational and deliberate acts like diary-writing, journaling, psychoanalysis and fiction-writing. For example, in *The Summer Before the Dark,* Kate achieves her self-reflective experience through her ongoing dreams, whereas in *The Golden Notebook* Anna achieves it through more deliberate acts like psychoanalysis, diary-writing and fiction-writing. Therefore, it is incorrect to affirm that Lessing fully rejects the rational modes of self-searching in favour of irrationality and spontaneity.

Lessing's works focus on her characters multiple *selves* and multiple voices. She also displays her characters' freedom to enter their inner selves, and create dialogues within them. They are also endowed with intuitive insights to perceive into their identity crises and inner breakdowns, so that they can lead their way into self-recovery and self-healing. For example, the present study has found how Anna and Kate achieve a quick insight into their inner breakdowns, and are frequently guided by the vivid serial dreams until they finally achieve self-healing.

The freedom that is offered to and enjoyed by Lessing's characters to enter their own selves has been found here as a therapeutic strategy explored by them for promoting intrapersonal interaction. Lessing's effort to project her characters' subjective experiences elucidates to her readers the naturally indefinite experience of self-recovery occurring within her characters' inner selves. The intrapersonal interaction created within the minds of characters is a distinct feature in writing, which is particularly and generally seen throughout Lessing's fiction. Lessing's characteristic narrative reflects her characters' multiple selves and the inner dialogues created among these selves. Her narrative style also projects how her characters achieve a divided self, of which one acts as an onlooker while fixing, observing and analysing other(s). The *Summer Before the Dark* and *The Golden Notebook* give ample evidences to verify the above. Kate Brown and Anna Woolf, the protagonists of the novel, achieve a quicker insight into their selves at crisis. Their inner journeys into their selves are guided by serialized mythical dreams invited at will. Similarly, they feel at ease to divide their selves and create inner dialogues between them.

Lessing has tried to evolve a similar line of intrapersonal experience in her autobiographies. It reflects her personal therapeutic intension behind her autobiographies that works in parallel to her character's personal therapeutic endeavours as pictured in her fictions. The three autobiographical works, *Under My Skin, Alfred and Emily,* and *The Memoirs of a Survivor* as analyzed in this study, offer plenty of instances where Lessing creates intrapersonal interaction within her mind through the medium of self-writing. She describes how she has attempted to divide her *self* in the first volume of autobiography, which lies close to Anna's attempt to divide herself in *The Golden Notebook.* Anna's attempt to erode the boundaries of writing and live through self-writing is much similar to that of Lessing's attempt in her autobiographies.

A comparison between Lessing's narrative technique in her autobiographies and her fictional works reveals the intrapersonal dialogues created within her as well as in her protagonists' minds. This confirms her strong belief that the individual can have an intuitive access into one's own psyche, realize one's own *self* in crisis, and lead oneself ahead towards self recovery. The interactional possibilities enabled within the intrapersonal realm that are created within her characters, and the same in Lessing's own mind, form the analyst-analysand pattern in psychotherapy. She emphasises how she employs one of her selves as a detached observer for fixing, analysing and healing her other selves that remain within her. It is the act of self-writing that enables her to pursue the possibility of exploring the analyst-analysand patterning.

Lessing's obsession with her own past and the lives of her parents reveal her deep interest in re-narrating and thereby exploring the traumatic events that occurred in her own life and her parents' lives. She also expresses her deep interest in analysing closely and resolving her own troubled relationship she had with her parents, particularly with her mother. The mother-daughter/mother-child relationships are significant motifs in her writing.

The analyst-analysand patterning is also found in her attempt at self-revision through self-writing. A strong criticism against her writing is her repetition, which is seen as a general nature of her writing, where similar themes recur. However, the present study views it as intentional – i.e. she plans it as a therapeutic strategy. A closer analysis of these repetitions reveals her attempts at therapeutic self-revisioning. While re-narrating and thereby re-analyzing a certain life event in her writing, she attempts such narrative revisioning that enables her to construct and reconstruct her *self,*by interpreting and reinterpreting a certain traumatic life event, developing alternative versions of the same, and choosing a healthier one to construct her *self* as a whole. A comparative analysis of these alternative versions in her autobiographical works reveals her purpose of using narrative revisioning for constructing a morally healthier version of a traumatic event, which is itself a self-healing act.

Lessing also explores therapeutic possibilities in interpersonal interactions, by exploring how the individual's self is affected by interpersonal relationships. She treats both self-constructive and self-destructive relationships, and tries to analyze the individual who experiences self-healing and self-disintegration. She also presents alternative relationships that the participants experience as therapeutic, by using them as compensatory to the disrupted relationships they had with certain people in the past. The present study has verified plenty of such instances that symbolically bring out relationships, where a participant transfers to the other his/her conflicted relationships. There are also instances in which one participant shares a stronger, motherly attachment with the other, where she experiences it as self-fulfilling. The narrator-Emily relationship in *The Memoirs of a Survivor*, Kate-Maureen attachment in *The Memoirs of a Survivor*, and Anna-Saul relationshipin The *Golden Notebook* enact mother-daughter/mother-child relationships. These relationships project the element of mutuality, a very significant characteristic of Lessing's self-constructive relationships. Thus, within the dyadic interpersonal realm, one participant achieves one's own self-discovery through the other. They engage in mutual analysis, in which one enables the self-discovery of the other. For example, in *The Memoirs of the Survivor* the narrator recognizes Emily's past as her own personal realm and then she achieves her own *self*-discovery in her attempt to discover Emily's past. In turn, Emily's self evolution is caused by her relationship with the narrator. The same pattern of mutuality can be seen in Emily-Hugo, Emily-June attachments. Similarly in *The Summer Before the Dark* (sic), the Kate-Maureen relationship can be viewed on the plane of mutuality. Kate's self-recovery is achieved within her dyadic relationship with Maureen, particularly in their shared attempt to construct Kate's self-story. Maureen plays the role of co-constructor in Kate's attempt to construct her self-story, and thereby she acts the role of an analyst. The element of mutuality is also so dominant inthe Anna-Saul relationship in *The Golden Notebook*. Anna surveys Saul's mind and analyses his inner breakdown and its roots. Her survey of Saul's mind opens up her own inner breakdown and its roots. Anna who plays the role of the analyst later takes the role of analysand just like Saul, whose role as the analysand is shifted to that of the analyst. In this way, the element of mutuality is the core of the therapeutic relationship established between Anna and Saul.

Thus, the complex interactional patterns in Lessing reveal several similarities to that of the analytic alliance in psychotherapy. By exploring these possibilities in writing she realise "self-healing" (GN 8). She is a writer who "lives to write". She insists: "I have to write: it's a neurosis. It's true. I get out of balance if I don't write" (Ingersoll 240).

Notes

1. Various terms have been used to represent the participants and their relationship in psychotherapy viz. 'doctor-patient relationship', 'analyst-analysand relationship' and 'client-therapist relationship'. The present study uses the last two terms interchangeably, and avoids the term 'doctor-patient relationship', which represents the medical model and remains as controversial as it dichotomizes the roles of the participants, by positioning the first participant (analyst) as more active, skilled, powerful, superior, and domineering than the second (analysand).

2. The term symbolizes a loose confederation of psychiatrists, psychologists, psychiatric nurses, social and welfare workers, lay people and so-called patients who oppose and offer a critique of 'traditional mental health practice and treatment'. They reject the traditional scientism and the deterministic thinking behind it, while accepting the notion of the existial 'phenomenology of experience. They stress the uniqueness of individual experience, and the subjective nature of 'reality', and thereby call for the rejection of the medical model concept of 'mental illness. The major contributors to anti-psychiatry are R.D Laing, Thomas Szasz and Peter Breggi.

3. The terms, 'self-writing', 'life-writing' and 'autobiographic writing' have been interchangeably used in this work. Helene Buss, an autobiographical theorist, is of the opinion that the terms, 'self-writing' and 'life-writing' would be more inclusive than the term 'autobiography' as they could represent all the sub-genres of autobiography (memoirs, confessions, journals and letters). She also points out how these two terms were more preferred by the Modern Language Association (Buss 5,13)

4. The term 'self-analysis' was introduced by Sandor Ferenczi. He proposed self-analysis and mutual analysis as challenges to the traditional limits of doctor-patient and analyst-analysand relationships (Fortune, *Mutual Analysis* 3)

5. In *Under My Skin* Lessing calls *The Memoirs* as her "dream autobiography": This idea of a dream autobiography became the world behind the wall in *the Memoirs of a Survivor* (UMS 29).

6. A master narrative is also called the 'dominant story' that dominates a person's concept of an ideal life story. This may obstruct the individual's urge to narrate his/her life story by influencing to think that his/her story is insignificant in relation to the dominant story, which is acceptable in the society (Freeman 122-36).

7. A school of psychoanalytic theory and therapy developed by Heinz Kohut. He defined psychological disorders in terms of the person's disrupted or unmet developmental needs, and he analyzed how early interactions between the infant and his caretakers decide the development of the infant's "self" and the infant's "self-objects"'. He maintained that parents' failure to empathize with their children and the responses of their children to these failures are the roots of almost all psychopathology. He saw that it is therapist's skill to empathize, and the strong bond between patient and therapist that work the curative factors (Norman 78-82).

8. The theory was formulated as a reaction against the Freudian conception of the child's libidinal tie to its mother, where he theorized need satisfaction as primary, and attachment as secondary or derived. The theory was developed by Bowlby and Ainsworth, who drew their concepts from ethology and developmental psychology. According to Bowlby "the infant and young child should experience a warm, intimate, and continuous relationship with his mother in which both find satisfaction and enjoyment" (qtd.in Bretherton 767). Ainsworth formulated the concept of maternal sensitivity to infant signals and its role in the development of infant-mother attachment patterns. Under attachment theory, a major goal in psychotherapy is the reappraisal of inadequate, outdated working models of self in relation to attachment figures, a particularly difficult task if important others, especially parents, have forbidden their review.

9. The terms, intersubjective and intersubjectivity, refer to the mutually shared psychoanalytic field created within the shared subjectivities of the analyst and the analysand in therapy. These terms were introduced by Object Relations theorists who drew their inspiration from Ferenczi's findings. Thus, psychoanalysis can no longer be considered as an

act of decoding and analyzing the structure of the analysand's internal world (intra-psychic and intra-subjective) as suggested by Freud (Green 18).

10. The terms, 'intersubjective' and 'intersubjectivity', refer to the mutually shared psycho-analytic field created within the shared subjectivities of the analyst and the analysand in therapy. These terms were introduced by Object Relations theorists who drew their inspiration from Ferenczi's findings. Thus, psychoanalysis can no longer be considered as an act of decoding and analyzing the structure of the analysand's internal world (intra-psychic and intra-subjective) as suggested by Freud (Green 18).

11. The term was introduced by Melanie Klein in her work Notes on some Schizoid Mechanisms. She states that the infant goes through a fantasy phase in which it projects its internal feelings to an external object by believing that the external object has qualities that are, in actuality, its own. Thus, the well-fed infant, filled with pleasure, turns this good feeling back onto the object and believes that the breast is good (Klein 99-110).

12. A term introduced by the Object Relations School to signify the unconscious act of an infant that defends itself by a fantasy process, imposing its own inner world on the fantasized external world and then 'reinternalising' this world. *Projective identification* involves on a fantasy level, which is the splitting off an unacceptable part of the self and sending that into the other object. Object-relations theorists consider the analyst as a vehicle onto which an internal object (a person, an aspect of a person, the self, or an aspect of the self) of the analysand is projected.

13. Ira Progoff (At a Journaling Workshop: The Basic Text and Guide for Using the Intensive Journal Process [1975]); Christina Baldwin (One to One: Self-Understanding through Journal Writing [1991]); Tristine Rainer (The New Diary: How to Use a Journal for Self-guidance and Expanded Creativity [1978].

14. "Autobiography (Part One): Impertinent Daughters" (1984) and

15. "Autobiography (Part Two): My Mother's Life"

16. Lessing's search into the truth behind her mother's personality is seen throughout her writing. In *Alfred and Emily* she strongly expresses this intention (AE 156).

17. Lessing compares two similar scenes of experience: the first, what her mother experienced

in front of her father, and the second, a similar one, which Lessing had in front her mother.

18. Markus and Nurious remark that choosing the 'desirable self' from the 'possible selves' is crucial in the act of self-recovery ("Possible Selves" 918-36). Self- recovery depends upon the person's ability to resist an 'undesirable possible self' and to achieve a 'desirable possible self' from the possible selves. The possible selves represent the integration of an individual's epistemic and motivational functions (923**).** They also reveal the individual's awareness of his/her motives and goals that are intricately connected to one's self-knowledge. An individual possesses a number of different personal motives, such as achievement motives and motives for affiliation.Markus proposes that a person may hold a number of possible selves that may include both the past the future selves. One's choice of past possible selves will define much of his/her future selves ("Possible Selves" 955). Constructing the past possible selves enables an individual to perceive potential selves he/she could become and would like to become (e.g., wealthy), or selves that would not be chosen (e.g., unemployed) (928-32).

19. A term used by R.D Laing in his work *Self and Others*. He describes how social groups operate by creating a kind of fantasy, which attracts the participants to join the groups without recognizing that they are sacrificing their individual identities. He also states how the social fantasy makes a person schizophrenic (*Self and Others* 24).

20. The fantasy of marriage is one of social fantasies as discussed by Laing (*Self and Others* 29)

21. Ella-Julia relationship is closely analyzed in the 'Yellow Notebook', and Anna's intention of writing it is to resolve her own emotional relationship with Molly. Later Anna gets dissatisfied with using fiction for analyzing her relationship with Molly, and chooses dairy for this purpose.

22. While part of Lessing's focus is centered on the individual's self in crisis, she also analyzes the individual who can achieve self-healing.

23. Psychoanalysis is one of the subjects treated in detail in the *The Golden Notebook* . For example, the novel presents the analytical interaction in detail. This is particularly clear in Anna's psychoanalytic sessions with Mrs. Marks (GN 450).

24. Anna-Saul pair enacts the transference relationship, which is the characteristic of the analyst-analysand alliance. Saul transfers to Anna his childhood conflicts with mother, while Anna transfers to Saul her own negative personality traits. In that way they get each other an insight into their unconscious conflicts (GN 555).

25. The concepts of relational psychoanalysis have been discussed in detail in the second chapter.

26. Lessing subtitled *The Memoirs of a Survivor* as *An Attempt at an Autobiography* (UMS 28). She also calls it "a dream autobiography" (UMS 29).

27. Opposite to her statement that *The Memoirs* is her autobiography, here Lessing calls it a novel (UMS 28-29).

28. *The Memoirs* fails to comply with Lejeune's 'autobiographic pact', which he uses as a yardstick for differentiating pure autobiography from its fictional variants such as 'autobiographical novel' and 'fictional autobiography' (Lejeune 13-14).

29. Freeman describes self-interpretation and self- rewriting as the two integrative acts in autobiography. He emphasizes that the past cannot be re-called as it was, rather the narrator retrieves his memory and constructs the past in accordance with the present context of his/her life (Freeman 49).

30. Lessing affirms this: "I used the nursery in Tehran, and the characters of my parents, both exaggerated and enlarged, because this is appropriate for the world of dreams" (UMS 29).

31. The realistic part of *The Memoirs* projects the self-evolution taking place within Emily. However, it often slides away from realism, with the narrator's descriptions of the spurt in Emily's physical growth.

Works Cited

Abbot, Porter H. *Diary Fiction.* Ithaca: Cornellop, 1984. Print.

Abrams, M. H, and Geoffrey Galt Harpham. *A Handbook of Literary Terms.* New Delhi: Cengage, 2009. Print.

Adams, J F. "Question as Interaction in Therapeutic Conversation." *Journal of Family Psychotherapy* 12.2 (1997): 17-35. print.

Anderson, Charles M, and Marian M. MacCurdy, eds. *Writing and Healing: Toward an Informed Practice.* Urbana: National Council of Teachers of English, 2000. Print.

Angus, Lynne E, and John Mc Leod, eds. *The Handbook of Narrative and Psychotherapy: Practice, Theory and Research.* California: Sage, 2004. Print.

Aron, Lewis. *A Meeting of Minds:Mutuality in Psychoanalysis.* London: The Analytic Press, 1996. Print.

Bretherton, Inge."The Origins of Attachment Theory: John Bowlby and Mary Ainsworth". *Developmental Psychology* 28 (1992): 759-775. Print.

Bruner, Gerome. "Life as a Narrative." *Social Research* 54 (1987): 13-32. Print.

Buss, Helen. "Writing and Reading Autobiographically." *Life Writing* 16.3 (1995): 5-15. Print.

Cederstrom, Loreli. *The Feminine Psyche: Jungian Patterns in the Novels of Doris Lessing.* NY: Peter Lang, 1990. Print.

Dooley, Gillian. "An Autobiography of Everyone? Intentions and Definitions in Doris Lessing's *The Memoirs of a Survivor*". *Life Writing Symposium,* 13-15 June, 2006. Print.

Drabble, Margaret. "Doris Lessing: Cassandra in a World under Siege". *Critical Essays on Doris Lessing.* Eds. Sprague and Tiger. Boston: G.K Hall, 1986. 50-54. Print.

Eakin, Paul John. *How Our Lives Become Stories: Making Selves.* NY: Cornell UP, 1999. Print.

Field, Michele. "Doris Lessing: Why Do We Remember?" *Publisher's Weekly* 19 Sept 1994: 47- 48. Print.

Fortune, Christopher John. "Editing the Sandor Ferenczi-George Groddeck Correspodence 1923 to1933". Diss.U of Toronto, 1996. Print.

---. *Mutual Analysis: a Logical Outcome of Sandor Ferenzi's Experiments in Psychoanalysis.* Ed. P. Rudnytsky. New York: NY University Press, 1998. Print.

Freeman, Mark. *Rewriting the Self: History, Memory and Narrative.* London: Routledge,1993. Print.

Freeman, Mark, and R.E Robinson. "The Development Within: an Alternative Approach to Study Lives". *New Ideas in Psychology* 8 (1990): 53-72. Print.

Giddens, Anthony. *Modernity and Self Identity: Self and Society in the Late Modern Age.* Oxford: Polity Press, 1991. Print.

Glendinning, Victoria. "The Return of She." *Times Literary Supplement*, 13 December 1974: 1403-1409. Print.

Green, Andre. *Psychoanalysis: a Paradigm for Clinical Thinking.* London: Free Association Books, 2002. Print.

Hazeleton, Lesley. "Doris Lessing on Feminism, Communism and Space Fiction." *New York Times* 25 July 1982. web. 20 June 2007.

Hester, Richard L. "Early Memory and Narrative Therapy." *Journal of Individual Psychology* 60.4 (2004):338-347. Print.

Holland, Norman N. "The Mind and the Book: A Long Look at Psychoanalytic Literary Criticism." *Psychoanalysis in Literature.* n.d. Web. 15 January 2013.

Howe, Irving. "Neither Compromise nor Happiness." *New Republic* (14 Dec 1962) 17. Print.

Hubert, Hermans. "The Self as a Theatre of Voices: Disorganization and Reorganization of a Position Repertoire." *Journal of Constructive Psychology* 19 (2006): 147-169. Print.

Ingersoll, Earl George, ed. *Doris Lessing Conversations.* Princeton: Ontario Review, 1994. Print.

Keitel, Evelyne. *Reading Psychosis: Readers, Texts and Psychoanalysis.* Oxford: Basil Black, 1989. Print.

Kerby, Anthony Paul. *Narrative and the Self.* Indiana: Bloomington, 1991. Print.

Klein, Melanie. "Notes on Some Schizoid Mechanisms". *International Journal of Psychoanalysis* 27 (1946): 99-110.Print.

Krouse, Tonya. "Freedom as Effacement in the *Golden Notebook*: Theorizing Pleasure, Subjectivity, and Authority". *Journal of Modern Literature* 29.3 (2006): 39-56. Print.

Kumar, Alka. *Doris Lessing: Journey in Evolution.* New Delhi: Books Plus, 2001. Print.

Laing, R.D. *Self and Others.* London: Tavistock, 1969. Print.

Lejeune, Philippe. *On Autobiography.* Ed. Paul John Eakin.Trans.Katherine Leary. Minneapolis: U of Minnesota, 1989. Print.

Lessing, Doris. "A Talk with Doris Lessing". *Doris Lessing: Conversations.* Minda Bikman. Ed. Earl G. Ingersoll. Princeton: Ontario Review Press, 1994. 61. Print.

---. *Alfred and Emily.* London: Harper Collins, 2008. Print.

---."Breaking down these Forms." *Putting the Questions Differently: Interviews with Doris Lessing.* Stephen Gray. Ed. Earl G. Ingersoll. London: Flamingo-Harper Collins, 1964-1994.109-19. Print.

---."Caged by the Experts." *Doris Lessing: Conversations.* Thomas Frick. Ed. Earl G. Ingersoll. Princeton: Ontario Review, 1994. 155- 68. Print.

---."The Inadequacy of the Imagination." *Doris Lessing: Conversations.* Jonah Raskin. Ed. Earl G. Ingersoll. Princeton: Ontario Review, 1994.13-18. Print.

---. *The Golden Notebook.* 1962. London: Flamingo, 1993. Print.

---. *The Memoirs of a Survivor.* London: Octagon, 1974. Print.

---.*Prisons We Choose to Live Inside.* Montreal: Canadian Broadcasting Corporation, 1986. Reprint, NY: Harper & Row, 1987. Print.

---. *The Summer Before the Dark.* London: Flamingo, 1973. Print.

---. "A Talk with Doris Lessing". *Doris Lessing: Conversations.* Minda Bikman. Ed. Earl G Ingersoll Princeton: Ontario Review Press, 1994. 61. Print.

---. "Talking as a Person." *Doris Lessing: Conversations.* Roy Newquist. Ed. Earl G. Ingersoll. Princeton: Ontario Review, 1994.3-12. Print.

---. *Under My Skin*: *Volume One of My Autobiography, to 1949.* London: Flamingo, 1995. Print.

---. "A Writer is not a Professor." *Doris Lessing: Conversations,* Jean-Maurice de Montremy. Ed. Earl G Ingersoll. Princeton: Ontario Review, 1994.193-99. Print.

---. "Writing as Time Runs Out." *Doris Lessing: Conversations,* Michael Dean. Ed. Earl G Ingersoll, Princeton: Ontario Review, 1994.193-99. Print.

Markus, Hazel, and Paula Nurious. "Possible Selves." *American Psychologist* 41 (1986): 954 - 969. Print.

Marlatt, Daphna. "Self-Representation and Fictionalysis." *Autographe* (1990): 13-17. Print.

Nalbantian, Suzanne. *Aesthetic Autobiography.* London: Macmillian, 1994. Print.

Norman, Levy A. "An Investigation into the Nature of Psychotherapeutic Process: A Preliminary Report". *Psychoanalysis and Social Process.* Ed. Jules.H Masserman. NY: Crune& Strattom, 1961. Print.

Ogden, T.H. "Reconsidering Three Aspects of Psychoanalytic Technique". *International Journal of Psychoanalysis* 77 (1996): 883-899. Print.

Pennebaker, James. *The Psychology of Physical Symptoms.* NY: Springer-Verlag, 1982. Print.

---."Tellling Stories: The Health Benefits of Narrative." *Literature and Medicine* 19.1 (2000): 3-18. Print.

Ricoeur, Paul. *Time and Narrative.* Chicago: U of Chicago Press 1984. Print.

Rose, Ellen Cronan. "Rev. of *Under My Skin: Volume One of My Autobiography to 1949,* by Doris Lessing". *Women 's Review of Books* 1 2.6 (1995): 11-12. Print.

Rousseau, Francois Olivier. "The Habit of Observing". *Doris Lessing: Conversations.* Ed. Earl G. Ingersoll Princeton: Ontario Review Press, 1994: 47-148. Print.

Rubenstein, Roberta. *The Novelistic Vision of Doris Lessing: Breaking the Forms of Consciousness.* Urbana:University of Illinois, 1979. Print.

Sacks, Elyn R. *Interperting Interpertation: The Limits of Hermeneutic Psychoanalysis.* Yale UP, 1999. Print.

Sacks, Oliver. *The Man Who Mistook His Wife for a Hat and Other Clinical Tales.* NY: Alfred A Knopf, 1986. Print.

Sage, Lorna. *Doris Lessing.* London: Methuen, 1983. Print.

Schafer, Roy. "Listening in Psychoanalysis." *Narrative* 13.3 (2005): n.pag.Web.7 June 2009.

---."Narration in the Psychoanalytic Dialogue." *Narrative* 13.2 (2005):
n.pag.Web.14 June 2009.

Simms, Karl. *Paul Recoeur.* Ed. Robert Eagleton. New York: Routledge, 2003. Print.

Smith, David Livingstone. Psychoanalysis in Focus. London: Sage, 2003. Print.

Spence, Donald. *The Freudian Metaphor Toward Paradigm Change in Psychoanalysis.* NY: Norton, 1987. Print.

Sprague, Claire, and Virginia Tiger, eds. *Critical Essays on Doris Lessing.*
Boston: GK Hall, 1986. Print.

Stevens, Anthony. *An Intelligent Person's Guide to Psychotherapy.* London: Gerald Duckworth, 1998. Print.

Stolerow, Robert D. *Contexts of Being; The Intersubjective Foundations of the Psychological Life.* NJ: The Analytic Press, 1992. Print.

Storr, Anthony. *Jung.* London: Collins, 1973. Print.

Sullivan, H. S. *The interpersonal theory of psychiatry.* New York: Norton, 1953. Print.

Taylor, Charles. *Sources of the Self: The Making of the Modern Identity.* Cambridge: Harvard UP, 1989. Print.

Vlastos, Marion. "Doris Lessing and R. D. Laing: Psychopolitics and Prophecy." *PMLA* 91.2 (1976): 245-57. Print.

Watkins, Susan. "Grande Dame or New Woman: Doris Lessing and the Palimpsest." *Literature Interpertation Theory* 17(2006): 243-52. Print.

Watzlawick, P, et al. *Pragmatics of Human Communication.* New York: Norton. 1967. Print.

Wellek, Rene, and Austin Warren. *Theory of Literature.* New York: Harcourt, 1942. Print.

White, Hayden. *Metahistory: The Historical Imagination in Nineteeth Centuary Europe.* Baltimore: Hopkis UP,1973. Print.

Wittaker, Ruth. *Doris Lessing.* London: Macmillian, 1998. Print.

Worthington, Kim L. *Self as Narrative: Subjectivity and Community in Contemporary Fiction.* NY: Oxford UP, 1996. Print.

Zinsser,William. *Inventing the Truth: The Art and Craft of Memoir.* Boston: Houghton Mifflin, 1995.Print.

Works Consulted

Abrams, M. H, and Stephen Greenblatt. *The Norton Anthology of English Literature.* New York: Norton, 2000. Print.

Adler, Alfred. *What Life Writing Should Mean to You.* NY: Capricorn, 1937. Print.

Arlene,Vetre, and Emilia Dowling. "Narrative Therapy with Children and their Families: a Practitioner's Guide to Concepts and Approaches." *Journal of Mental Health* 15.3 (2006): 371. Print.

Armstrong, Nancy. *Desire and Domestic Fiction: A Political History of the Novel.* New York: Oxford University Press, 1987. Print.

Aron, Lewis. "The Paradoxical Place of Enactment in Psychoanalysis: Introduction." *Psycholanalytic Dialogues* 13.5 (2003): 623-631. Print.

Bakhurst, Sypnowich, and David Christine, eds. *The Social Self.* London: Sage, 1995. Print.

Bentley, Nick. "Doris Lessing's *The Golden Notebook*: An Experiment in Critical Fiction". *Doris Lessing: Border Crossings.* Eds. Alice Ridout and Susan Watkins. London: Continuum, 2009. 44-60. Print.

Bluck, Susan. "Life Experience with Death: Relation to Death Attitudes to the Use of Death Related Memories." *Death Studies* 32 (2008): 524-549. Print.

Boehm, Beth. "Re-educating Readers: Creating New Expectations for *The Golden Notebook*."*Narrative* 5.1 (1997): 88-97. Print.

Bonaparte, Marie. *Étude Psychanalytique.* Paris: Denöel et Steele, (1933). Print.

Brickman, Celia. "Primitivity, Race, and Religion in Psychoanalysis." *The Journal of Religion* 82.1 (2002): 53-74. Print.

Butte, George. "I know that I know that I know: Reflections on Paul John Eakin's 'What We Read in Autobiography'". *Narrative* 13.3 (2005): 299-306. Print.

Byatt, A. S. *A Whistling Woman.* New York: Alfred A. Knopf, 2002. Print.

Canary, Robert H, and Henry Kozicki, eds. *The Writing of History: Literary Form and Historical Understanding.* Madison: University of Wisconsin Press, 1978. Print.

Chaffee, Patricia. "Spatial Patterns and Closed Groups in Lessing's African Stories."*South Atlantic Quarterly* 43.2 (1978): 126-32. Print.

Chennells, Anthony. "Postcolonialism and Doris Lessing's Empires." *Doris Lessing Studies* 21.2 (2001): 4-11. Print.

Coetzee, J. M . "The Heart of Me." Rev. of *Under My Skin. New York Review of Books.* n.pag. Web. 22 Feb. 2008.

Damasio, Antonio. *Descartes' Error: Emotion, Reason, and the Human Brain.* New York: G. P. Putnam's Sons, 1994. Print.

David, Cooper. *The Language of Madness.* London: Penguin, 1978. Print.

Dimaggio, Giancarlo. "Disorganized Narratives in Clinical Practice." *Journal of Constructive Psychology* 19 (2006): 103-108. Print.

Draine, Betsy. *Substance under Pressure: Artistic Coherence and Evolving Form in the Novels of Doris Lessing.* Madison: University of Wisconsin Press, 1983. Print.

Du Plessis, Rachel Blau. "For the Etruscans." *Feminist Criticism: Essays on Women, Literature, and Theory.* Ed. Elaine Showalter. New York: Pantheon, 1985. 271-9. Print.

Eakin, Paul John."Selfhood, Autobiography, and Interdisciplinary Enquiry: A Reply to George Butt." *Narrative* 13.3 (2005): 307-311. Print.

---. "What are We Reading when We Read Autobiography." *Narrative* 12.2 (2004) 88-94. Print.

Fand, Roxanne. *The Dialogic Self: Reconstructing Subjectivity in Woolf, Lessing, and Atwood.* Selinsgrove, PA: Susquehanna University Press, 1999. Print.

Fanon, Frantz. *The Wretched of the Earth.* Trans. Constance Farrington. New York: Grove Press, 1966. Print.

Farwell, Marilyn R. "Virginia Woolf and Androgyny." *Contemporary Literature* 16.4 (1975): 433-51. Print.

Fernades, Fatima. "A Response to Erila Burman." *Journal of Psychotherapy, Counselling and Health* 6.4 (2003): 309-316. Print.

Fishburn, Katherine. "Teaching Doris Lessing as a Subversive Activity: A Response to the Preface to *The Golden Notebook*." *Alchemy.* Eds. Carey Kaplan, and Ellen Cronan Rose. New York: MLA, 1989. 81-92. Print.

---. *The Unexpected Universe of Doris Lessing: A Study in Narrative Technique.* Westport, CT: Greenwood, 1985. Print.

---. "Worlds within Words: Doris Lessing as Meta-Fictionist and Meta-Physician." *Studies in the Novel* 20.2 (1988): 186-205. Print.

Freeman, Mark, and R.E Robinson. "Why Narrative? Hermeneutics, Historical Understanding, and the Significance of Stories." *Journal of Narrative and Life History* 7 (1997): 169-176. Print.

Freud, Sigmund. *General Introduction to Psychoanalysis.*Trans. G.Stanley Hall. London,1987. Print.

Friedman, Ellen G, and Miriam Fuchs. *Breaking the Sequence: Women's Experimental Fiction.* Princeton, NJ: Princeton University Press, 1989. Print.

Friedman, Susan Stanford. *Women's Autobiographical Selves: Theory and Practice.* Ed. Insheri Benstock. Chapel Hill: U of North Carolina Press, 1988. Print.

Galin, Muge. *Between East and West: Sufism in the Novels of Doris Lessing.* Albany: State University of New York Press, 1997. Print.

Gardiner, Judith Kegan."Historicizing Homophobia in *The Golden Notebook* and 'The Day Stalin Died'". *Doris Lessing Studies* 25.2 (2006): 14-18. Print.

Gasiorek, Andrzej. *Post-War British Fiction: Realism and After.* London: Edward Arnold, 1995. Print.

Gergen, Kenneth J. *The Structured Self: Dilemmas of Identity in Contemporary Life.* NY: Basic Books, 1985. Print.

---. *Realities and Relationships.* Cambridge: Harvard UP, 1994. Print.

Greene, Gayle. *Changing the Story: Feminist Fiction and the Tradition.* Bloomington: Indiana University Press, 1991. Print.

Hammer, Emmanuel. F. *Use of Interpertation in Treatment: Technique and Art.* NY: Grune&Stratton, 1968. Print.

Hanson, Clare. "Doris Lessing in Pursuit of the English; or, No Small, Personal Voice." *PN Review* 14.4 (1987): 39-42. Print.

Hartman, Geoffrey. *The Interpreter's Freud.* Eds.David Lodge and Nigel Wood. New Delhi: Pearson Education, 1998. Print

Head, Dominic. *The Cambridge Companion to Modern British Fiction, 1950-2000.* Cambridge: Cambridge UP, 2002. Print.

Henster, Sarah. "Nuclear Cassandra: Prophesy in Doris Lessing's *The Golden Notebook*." *Papers on Language& Literature* 43.1 (2007): n.pag.Web. 8 Nov 2009.

Hite, Molly. "Doris Lessing's *The Golden Notebook* and *The Four-Gated City:* Ideology, Coherence, and Possibility." *Twentieth Century Literature* 34.1 (1988): 16-29. Print.

---. *The Other Side of the Story: Structures and Strategies of Contemporary Feminist Narrative.* Ithaca, NY: Cornell University Press, 1989. Print.

Holland, Norman N. "The Mind and the Book: A Long Look at Psychoanalytic Literary Criticism." *Psychoanalysis in Literature*. n.d. Web. 15 January 2013.

Hubert, Hermans. "The Innovation of Self-narratives: a Dialogical Approach". *The Handbook on Narrative and Psychotherapy: Practice, Theory and Research*. Eds. Lynne E. Angus and John Mc Leod. California: Sage *Publications*, 2004:175-191. Print.

Hutcheon, Linda. "The Pastime of Past Time: Fiction, History, Historiographic Metafiction." *Genre* 20 (1987): 285-305. Print.

Iser, Wolfgang. *The Implied Reader: Patterns of Communication in Prose Fiction from Bunyan to Beckett. Baltimore*: Johns Hopkins UP, 1980. Print.

James, Strachey. "Some Unconscious Factors in Reading". *International Journal of Psychoanalysis* 31 (1930): 322-333. Print.

James, Thomson. A, and Nancy Richardson. "The Effect of Autobiogaphical Writing on the Subjective Well-being of Older Adults." *North American Journal of Psychology* 4.3 (2002): 395- 404. Print.

Jones, Earnest. *Hamlet and Oedipus.* NY: Norton, 1910. Print.

Jordan, Judith. "Empathy and Self Boundaries." *The Women and Language Debate: A Sourcebook*. Eds. Camille Roman et al. NJ: Rutgers University Press, 1994. 153-64. Print.

Kaivola, Karen. "Revisiting Woolf's Representations of Androgyny: Gender, Race, Sexuality, and Nation." *Tulsa Studies in Women's Literature* 18.2 (1999): 235-61. Print.

Kaplan, Carey, and Ellen Cronan Rose, eds. *Approaches to Teaching Lessing's The Golden Notebook*. NY: MLA, 1989. Print.

Keylor, Rheta G. "Subjectivity, Infantile Oedipus and Symbolization in Malanie Klein and Jaques Lacan". *Psychoanalytic Dialogues* 13.2 (2003): 211-242. Print.

King, Jeanette. *Doris Lessing.* London: Edward Arnold, 1989. Print.

Klein, Carole. *Doris Lessing.* London: Duckworth, 2000. Print.

La Capra, Dominick. *Writing History, Writing Trauma.* Baltimore: John Hopkins University Press, 2001. Print

Laing, R.D. *The Divided Self.* London: Penguin, 1960. Print.

---. *The Politics of Experience.* NY: Pantheon Random,1967. Print.

Leod, John Mc. *Narrrative and Psychotherapy.* London: Sage, 1997. Print.

Leonard, John. 'The Spacing out of Doris Lessing." *New York Times Book Review* 7 Feb 1982: 1, 34-35. Print.

Lessing, Doris. *African Laughter: Four Visits to Zimbabwe.* NY: Harper Collins, 1992. Print.

---. *Briefing for a Descent to Hell.* London: Flamingo, 1971. Print.

---. "A Conversation with Doris Lessing." Interview by Billy Gray. *Doris Lessing Studies* 24.1 and 2 (2004): 1, 23-30. Print.

---. *The Diaries of Jane Somers.* NY: Vintage Books, 1984. Print.

---. *The Four-Gated City.* London: Granada, 1983. Print.

---. *Going Home.* London: Granada, 1968. Print.

---. *The Habit of Loving.* NY: Thomas Y. Crowell, 1957. Print.

---. "An Interview with Doris Lessing." Interview by Susan Stamberg. *Doris Lessing Newsletter* 8.2 (Fall 1984): 3-4, 15. Print.

---. *Landlocked.* St. Albans, Herts: Panther-Granada, 1973. Print.

---. *Love Again.* London: Flamingo, 1995. Print.

---. "The Need to Tell Stories." *Putting the Questions Differently: Interviews with Doris Lessing.* Christopher Bigsby. Ed. Earl G Ingersoll. London: Flamingo-Harper Collins, 1964-1994.70-85. Print.

---. "The Small Personal Voice." 1957. *A Small Personal Voice,* ed. Paul Schlueter, NY: Vintage, 1974, 3-21. Print.

---. *Time Bites: Views and Reviews.* London, NY: Harper Collins, 2004. Print.

---. "Voice of England, Voice of Africa." *Doris Lessing: Conversations.* Michael Upchurch. Ed. Earl G. Ingersoll. Princeton: Ontario Review, 1994. 219-27. Print.

---. *Walking in the Shade: Volume Two of My Autobiography, 1949 to 1962.* NY: Harper Collins, 1997. Print.

---. "Watching the Angry and Destructive Hordes Go Past." *Doris Lessing: Conversations.* Claire Tomalin. Ed. Earl G Ingersoll. Princeton: Ontario Review, 1994. 173-77. Print.

Levenson, O Ada. *20th Centuary Fiction.* Ed. James Vinson. Hong Kong: Macmillian, 1983. Print.

Lightfoot, Marjorie. *The Golden Notebook as a Modernist Novel: Approach to Teaching Lessing's The Golden Notebook.* Eds. Carely Kapla and Ellen Cronan Rose. NY: MLA,1989. Print.

Likerman, Meira. "Reviews Malanie Klein: Her Work in Context." *Journal of Child Psychology* 28.2 (2002):255-260. print.

Mahony, Patric. *Psychoanalysis and Discourse.* London: Tavistock Publication, 1987. Print.

Maroda.K.J. *The Power of Counter Transference: Innovations in Analytic Techenique.* Chichester: John Wiley, 1991. Print.

Maslen, Elizebeth. *Doris Lessing.* Plymoth: Northcoast Publishers, 1994. Print.

Mayo, Joseph A. "Using Mini-Autobiogaphical Narration in Applied Psychology to Personalize Course Conceptual Application." *Jornal of Constructivist Psychology* 17 (2004): 237- 246. Print.

Mehlman, Jeffry. *A Structural Study of Autobiography: Proust, Leiris, Satre, Levi-Strauss.* Ithaca: Cornell University, 1974. Print.

Merendino, Rosario."The Psychoanalytical Field of Interpretation." *Psychomedia* 5 (1997).Web. 27 Aug 2006. Print.

Michael, Magali Cornier. *Feminism and the Postmodern Impulse: Post-World War II Fiction.* Albany: State University of New York Press, 1996. Print.

Miller, J. Hillis. "The Problematic Ending in Narrative." *Nineteenth-Century Fiction* 33.1 (1978): 3-7. Print.

Minh-ha, Trinh T. *Woman, Native, Other: Writing Postcoloniality and Feminism.* Bloomington: Indiana University Press, 1989. Print.

Morgan, Ellen. "Alienation of the Woman Writer in *The Golden Notebook*". *Doris Lessing: Critical Studies.* Eds. Annis Pratt, and Dembo L. S. Madison: University of Wisconsin Press, 1974.54-63. Print

Muran, J.D, and Safran J.D. *Negotiating the Therapeutic Alliance.* NY: Guilford Press, 2000. Print.

Neimeyer, Robert A. *Narrative Disruption and the Construction of the Self.* Ed. Neimyer R and J. Ruskin. Washington: APA, 2000. Print.

---."Chaos to Coherence: Psychotherapeutic Integration of Traumatic Loss." *Journal of Constructivist Psychology* 19 (2006): 127-145. Print.

---. "Narrating the Dialogical Self: Toward an Expnanded Tool Box for the Counselling Psychologist." *Counselling Psychology* 19.1 (2006): 105-120. Print.

Olney, James. *Memory and Narrrative in the Weave of Life-Writing. Chicago*: U of Chicago Press, 1999. Print.

Pennebaker, James. "Confession, Inhibition and Desease." *Experimental Psychology* 22 (1989): 211- 244. Print.

---. *Opening Up.* NY: Guilford Press, 1990. Print.

Perrakis, Phyllis Sternberg, ed. *Adventures of the Spirit: The Older Woman in the Works of Doris Lessing, Margaret Atwood, and Other Contemporary Women Writers* Columbus: The Ohio State University Press, 2007. Print.

---. "Doris Lessing's *The Golden Notebook:* Separation and Symbiosis." *American Imago* 38.4 (1981): 407-28. Print.

---. "The Marriage of Inner and Outer Space in Doris Lessing's *Shikasta.*" *Science-Fiction Studies* 17.2 (July, 1990): 221-38. Print.

---. "Navigating the Spiritual Cycle in *Memoirs of a Survivor* and *Shikasta*." *Adventures of the Spirit: the Older Woman in the Works of Doris Lessing, Margaret Atwood, and Other Contemporary Women Writers*. Ed. Phyllis Sternberg Perrakis. Columbus: The Ohio State University Press, 2007. 47-82. Print.

---. ed. *Spiritual Exploration in the Works of Doris Lessing*. Westport, CT: Greenwood Press, 1999. Print.

---. "Sufism, Jung and the Myth of Kore: Revisionist Politics in Lessing's *Marriages*" *Mosaic: A Journal for the Interdisciplinary Study of Literature* 25.3 (1992): 99-120. Print.

Pickering, Jean. "Philosophical Contexts for *The Golden Notebook*". *The Alchemy of Survival*. Eds. Carey Kaplan and Ellen Cronan Rose. Athens: Ohio University Press, 1988. 43-49. Print.

Pratt, Annis, and L.S. Dembo, eds. *Doris Lessing: Critical Studies.* Madison:University of Wisconsin Press, 1974. Print.

Pitt, Alice. "Reading Women's Autobiography: on the Loss and Redefining the Mother." *Changing English* 11.2 (2004). Print.

Rapping, Elayne Antler. "Unfree Women: Feminism in Doris Lessing's Novels." *Women's Studies* 3 (1975): 29-44. Print.

Raschke, Debrah. "Cabalistic Gardens: Lessing's *Memoirs of a Survivor: Spiritual Exploration in the Works of Doris Lessing*. Ed. Phyllis Sternberg Perrakis. CT: Greenwood Press, 1999. 43-54. Print.

---. *Modernism, Metaphysics, and Sexuality.* Selinsgrove, PA: Susquehanna University Press, 2006. Print.

Restuccia, Frances L. "'Untying the Mother Tongue': Female Differences in Virginia Woolf's *A Room of One's Own.*" *Tulsa Studies in Women's Literature* 4.2 (1985): 253-64. Print.

Renik,Owen. "Analytic Interaction: Conceptualizing Techniques in the Light of the Analyst's Irreducible Subjectivity". *Relational Psychoanalysis: The Emergence of a Tradition.* Eds. S.A Mitchell, and L. Aron. NJ: Analytic Press, 1993. Print.

Ronald, Kellong T. *The Psychology of Writing.* NY: Oxford UP, 1994. Print.

Roy, Pascal. *Design and Truth in Autobiography.* London: Routledge, 1960. Print.

Rubenstein, Roberta. "An Evening at the 92 Street Y." *Doris Lessing News Letter* 2 (1984): Print.

---. *Home Matters: Longing and Belonging, Nostalgia and Mourning in Women's Fiction.* New York: St. Martin's Press, 2001. Print.

---. "Martha Still Questing: Reading *Mara and Dann* through *Children of Violence.*" *Doris Lessing Newsletter* 21.1 (2000): 10-13. Print.

---. "Notes for Proteus: Doris Lessing Reads the Zeitgeist." *Doris Lessing: Integrating the Times*, Eds. Debrah Raschke et. al. Columbia: Ohio State University Press, 2010.11-31. Print.

---. "*The Marriages between Zones Three, Four, and Five:* Doris Lessing's Alchemical Allegory." *Critical Essays on Doris Lessing.* Eds. Claire Sprague and Virginia Tiger. Boston: GK Hall, 1986. 60-68. Print.

Sarah, Henstra. "Nuclear Cassandra: Prophesy in Doris Lessing's *The Golden Notebook.*" *Papers on language and Literature* 11.2 (2003): n.pag. Web. 14 July 2009.

Saxton, Ruth, and Jean Tobin, eds. *Woolf and Lessing: Breaking the Mold.* NY: St. Martin's Press, 1994. Print.

---, ed. *A Small Personal Voice: Essays, Reviews, Interviews.* NY: Vintage, Print.

Schafer, Roy . *Retelling Life: Narration and Dialogue in Psychoanalysis.* NY: Basic Books, 1992. Print.

---."Who's Here: Thoughts on Narrative Identity and Narrative Imperialism." *Narrative* 13.3 (2005):n.pag. Web. 4 June 2009. Print.

Schiwy, Marlenea. *A Voice of Her Own: Women and the Journal Writing Journey.* NY: Fireside, 1948. Print.

Schlucter, Paul. "Self-Analytic Women".*The Golden Notebook.* Ed. Harold Bloom. NY: Chelsea, 1988. 88-96. Print.

---. "Review of *Love, Again.*" *Doris Lessing Newsletter* 18.1 (1996): 1, 6. Print.

Scott, Lynda. "Writing the Self: Selected Works of Doris Lessing." *Deep South* 2.2 (1996): n.pag. Web. 4 Feb 2007.

Seagal, J, and James W Pennebacker. "Forming a Story : The Health Benefits of Narrrative." *Journal of Clinical Psychology* 55 (1999): 1243-1254. Print.

Shane, Estelle. "Discussion of Joseph Newirth's Paper and the Eroticized Transference-Counter Transference." *Psychoanalytic Inquiry* 25.3 (2005): Web. n.pag. 18 Dec 2005.

Shane.M, et al. *Intimate Attachments: Toward a Self Psychology.* NY: Gilford Press, 1997. Print.

Shah, Idries. *The Sufis.* London: Octagon, 1964. Print.

Showalter, Elaine. *The Female Melady: Women, Madness, and English Culture,* 1830-1980. NY: Penguin,1987. Print.

Spence, Donald. P. *Narrative Truth and Historical Truth.* NY: Norton, 1984. Print.

Spengeman, William C. *The Forms of Autobiography: Episodes in the History of a Literary Genre.* New Haven: Yale University, 1980. Print.

Sprague, Claire. "Doubletalk and Doubles Talk in *The Golden Notebook.*" *Papers on Language and Literature: A Journal for Scholars and Critics of Language and Literature* 18.2 (1982): 181-97. Print.

---. *"The Golden Notebook:* In Whose or What Great Tradition?" *Approaches to Teaching Lessing's The Golden Notebook.* Eds. Carey Kaplan, and Ellen Cronan Rose. New York: The Modern Language Association, 1989. 78-83. Print.

---, ed. *In Pursuit of Doris Lessing: Nine Nations Reading.* New York: St. Martin's Press, 1990. Print.

---. "Lessing's *The Grass is Singing, Retreat to Innocence, The Golden Notebook* and Eliot's *The Waste Land.*" *Explicator* 50.3 (1992): 177-80. Print.

---. "Multipersonal and Dialogic Modes in *Mrs. Dalloway* and *The Golden Notebook.*" Ed. Ruth Saxton and Jean Tobin, *Woolf and Lessing,* 3-14. Print.

---. *Re-Reading Doris Lessing: Narrative Patterns of Doubling and Repetition.* Chapel Hill: University of North Carolina Press, 1987. Print.

Strauss, Claude Levi. *Structural Anthropology.* Trans. Claire Jacobson and Brooke Grudfest Schoept. Harmondworth: Penguin, 1968. Print.

Sullivan, Henry. S. *Conceptions of Modern Psychiatry.* NY: Norton, 1940. Print.

---. *The Interpersonl Theory of Psychiatry.* New York: Norton, 1953. Print.

Tanlim et al. "The Older I get the Less I Believe." *Doris Lessing Conversations.* Ed. Earl G. Ingersoll.Princeton: Ontario Review Press, 1994. Print.

Terry, Paul. "Working with Psychosis Part I: Grieving the Damage of Psychotic Illness." *Psychodynamic Practice* 10:1 (2003): 63-71. Print.

Tiger, Virginia. "Made from Memories." *Doris Lessing Studies* 22.2 (2002): 1, 8-10, 24. Print.

Wallace, Diana. "Women's Time: Women, Age, Intergenerational Relationships in Doris Lessing's the Diaries of Jane Somers." *Studies in Literary Imagination* 39.2(2006): 110-118. Print.

White, Hayden. *Metahistory: The Historical Imagination in Nineteeth Centuary Europe.* Baltimore: Hopkis UP,1973. Print.

White, Michael, and David Epston. *Narrrative Means to Therapeutic Ends.* NY: Norton, 1984. Print.